AF290998

wiggle room

Supporting Role
Jason Hirata

wiggle room # 2

Supporting Role
by Jason Hirata

Wiggle Room #2

Reliable Copy #14
First Edition - 1000

Series Editors: Nihaal Faizal and
Sarasija Subramanian
Copy Editor: Press Works
Design: Nihaal Faizal

All images are courtesy of the author.

*Cover Image: Different Telling of the Same
Story* by Jason Hirata, 2016
Metal shelf, 86 x 35 ½ inches
Installation view from *Plot* by Tony Chrenka
and Jason Hirata at Theta, New York, 2021.

Printed by Pragati Offset, Hyderabad

ISBN: 978-81-970506-3-3

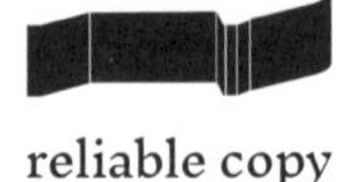

Jason Hirata and Reliable Copy would like to thank 80WSE, AlliiertenMuseum, Arias Alea, Gianmaria Andreetta, Tamara Antonijević, Lutz Bacher, Alessio Baldissera, Amelia Bande, Noah Barker, Alex Bienstock, Hannah Black, Boško Blagojević, Matt Browning, Brücke-Museum, Gloria de Risi, Dora Budor, John Burkhart, Wisrah C. V. da R. Celestino, Domingo Castillo, Tony Chrenka, Stella Cillman, Lorel Easterbrooks, Edilmanca, Fanta-MLN, Hannah Feldman, Alex Fleming, Jim Fletcher, Michèle Graf, Adjua Gargi Nzinga Greaves, Selina Grüter, Rachel Haidu, Markus Hannebauer, Trajal Harrell, fields harrington, Saidiya Hartman, Emma Hedditch, Blaise Hirata, Debbe Hirata, Gobe Hirata, Ken Hirata, Moritz Hirsch, Jon Huron, Flint Jamison, Cornelia Kastelan, Adam Khalil, Zack Khalil, Svetlana Kitto, Anya Komar, KOW, Kunsthalle Basel, Kunst Halle Sankt Gallen, Pope.L, Nicola Lees, Hongzhe Liang, Sean Lockwood, Jason Loebs, Jordan Lord, Balthazar Lovay, Zoey Lubitz, Zoey Marks, Park McArthur, Christian Philipp Müller, Vreni Naess, Paolo Nava, New Red Order, Minh Nguyen, No Total, Nia Nottage, Christian Kōun Alborz Oldham, Nicholas Pittman, Jackson Polys, Lucas Quigley, Nick Raffel, Margherita Raso, Regards,, David Robbins, Carissa Rodriguez, Anna Rubin, Sydney Schrader, Mike Schuh, Natalie Popovic Schuh, Noam Segal, NCC Milano Services, Richard Sides, Artists Space, Stadtgalerie Bern, Hito Steyerl, Nick Strobelt, Cornice Studio, Knut Olaf Sunde, Milan Ther, Elisa Tinterri, Christopher Weickenmeier, Ivo Wessel, Angharad Williams, Satsuma Wong, Alex Wong, Chris Wu, and Alberto Zenere.

Contents

Editors' Note
Sometimes You're Both

A practice performs. It performs and it enacts, and in enacting it develops a language through which it builds, affirms, utters, iterates, and clarifies itself. For decades, the idea of art as language had been about a way of reading a work of art, through its pictorial or material qualities.[1] However, in practice, language can be much more than pictorial signs and material signifiers. It can be a set of methods, repeated strategies, recurring figures—all that gives an artistic output a consistency, a shape, and form.

The artist Marcel Duchamp (1887-1968) best points the way to this broader position, through his restless engagement with both art and language.[2] What he makes abundantly clear is that language serves a purpose, is essential and inevitable, but that it also comes with certain limits. Sometimes as soon as one's language is carefully delineated, it starts to impose itself, it becomes an obstacle. And so, one must learn to speak in different tongues.

This series, titled Wiggle Room, is our editorial attempt at bringing together practices that emerge against the limits of artistic predetermination—that push against it, charting new positions, new roles, new figures; simultaneously building a language and thwarting it. These are practices that challenge the usual confines of the art context, causing a leak, a seepage. Often these are elusive, not enacting ruptures or revolutions, not loud proclamations, but just a slight wave of the hand—a simple magic trick. On these occasions, they come close to Duchamp's concept of the 'infrathin', undefinable except by its examples: the warmth of a seat that has just been left, the whistling sound made by velvet trousers, or tobacco smoke that smells also of the mouth which exhaled it.

And so, with Wiggle Room, we engage in a kind of mapping—not formal, nor necessarily comprehensive, definitely not territorial, but one where practices and positions come gently into view. We trace coordinates, we explore options, we plot escapes. And for this, we look no further for guidance than to the artists themselves, presenting them here in their own words—making room for a verbal articulation of these not-quite-literal languages. In Wiggle Room #1, we presented the artist David Robbins and his bringing-together of art and entertainment as a way towards a wider context and audience for one's cultural productions. David often speaks of art as a demonstration of freedom, something that he himself illustrates in his decades-long practice: shifting gears, broadening the field, and even (when necessary) dropping out altogether.

Linked undeniably to this demonstration of freedom, is support. As independent as a practice may claim to be, it is always propped up, whether in terms of knowledge (coordinates—canonical or obscure), resources (affordances—financial or practical), or context (opportunities—professional or personal). A demonstration of freedom then, is really a demonstration of support.

In his practice, across video, sculpture, photography, and text, Jason Hirata often demonstrates support. Sometimes this takes the form of a joke, a push, or a hand. Sometimes it is a gentle lean, like when he borrows piss bottles from the city of New York, only to return them once again to its streets (*Why Not Lie?*, 2020). Sometimes it is weightier, like caregiving and attending, or using his partner's wheelchair as a power tool to flatten metal racks (*Different Telling of the Same Story*; *Upstairs Neighbor*; and *Rack*, all 2016).

Support can mean all kinds of things—to underpin or reinforce, hold or carry; it can mean involvement or participation, endorsement or sponsorship. It can be a doing or a receiving, an aid or a role, passive or active, contingent on context, dependency, and need. It can even be 'infrathin'—an event hovering at the edge of difference, barely perceptible, dancing in and out of view.

Growing up in Seattle, Jason studied art at the University of Washington. His mother Debbe Hirata is a voiceover artist, who Jason sometimes assists with recording and editing. After graduating, to earn a living, Jason produced documentation videos for museums and art spaces, while also assisting with installing shows and producing exhibitions. He also began working for other artists including Jason Loebs, Carissa Rodriguez, and Hito Steyerl. He was employed by Lutz Bacher as her studio assistant for two years, and works such as *Floaters*, 2020 (a work comprised of numerous borrowed projectors displaying test screens of an identical hue), came from infrastructures afforded by these moments of access to other artists' tools and resources.

Though support comes in many forms, it is often visible only when activated as an action—whether as a lean or a push, a stretch or a prop. And so, Jason's early solo exhibitions largely featured works by other artists, as well as non-artists, comprising those productions in which he had played a lending hand, a supporting role. As the title of one of these shows articulated, *sometimes you're both*[3]—artist and assistant, mind and body, thought and action, practice and language, caregiver and dependent. His practice today continues to enact support, though now in more complex forms such as loaning money to his gallery (*The Borrowers*, 2022), contributing texts for other artists' exhibitions, and also through teaching—a role he performs with his partner Park McArthur.

Assembled in this book, as Wiggle Room #2, is a selection of Jason's writings from 2019 to the present. Similar to his artworks, these texts demonstrate a role, they perform a language. They are all in support of something—an exhibition, an invitation, another artist's practice, and they are shyly epistolary: not quite diary entries or letters, but checklists, press releases, visual descriptions, exhibition reviews, invoices, and curricula vitae. They are texts built from the supporting documents of an artistic practice and presentation, while simultaneously offering further support.

While working on the book's selection, Jason emailed us the following: "writing is the process, text is the product." What's collected here in this book is something in between. Not entirely form, not fully process—but something that leans, that lends, that props, that aids, that wiggles. Something that performs two roles simultaneously, much like Jason's practice. Something that's both.

[1] In India, this lesson is largely attributed to KG Subramanyan, who himself took from EH Gombrich, whose lectures he attended as a student of Slade School of Fine Art between 1955-56.

[2] Joseph Kosuth was first to articulate this in his essay 'Art After Philosophy' (1969): "Another way of putting it would be that art's 'language' remained the same, but it was saying new things. The event that made conceivable the realisation that it was possible to 'speak another language' and still make sense in art was Marcel Duchamp's first unassisted readymade."

[3] 'Sometimes You're Both' was first a title that Jason gave Park McArthur for a work in 2016. Later it was borrowed by Jason as the title of his exhibition at 80WSE, New York in 2019. In the spirit of lending, it has been borrowed once again, this time by the editors as the title for this introductory note.

25 OCTOBER, 2015 — 12 MAY, 2019 (2019)

kunstvereinnuernberg.de
T. +49 (0) 911 241 562
F. +49 (0) 911 241 563
Kressengartenstraße 2
90402 Nürnberg

28. Februar 2019

I have never looked at all of these objects in the same place before. These works aren't mine, yet the exhibition is my solo show.

To make a living I do various technical jobs in the field of art in New York City. I work as an assistant to artists. I make videos. I install exhibitions. My partner is an artist and I often help her in the studio, as she helps me. Many of my friends are artists too and their practices almost always require collective action at some point. I also work for people who *don't* make art, but nonetheless require the production of material content. This activity occupies a large part of my time so that most of my days are spent in the space of other people's practices. I play a support role in these activities, and sometimes a catalytic one. Occasionally, I am there to do something unexpected.

25 October, 2015—12 May, 2019 is an exhibition of works that have been loaned to me and result from these relationships. It presents some of my commitments over the last five years. It traces my activity and engagement, and gives form to a variety of supporting roles.

— Jason Hirata

25 OCTOBER, 2015 — 12 MAY, 2019

Lutz Bacher, Alex Bienstock, Dora Budor, Matt Browning, Lorel Easterbrooks, Jim Fletcher, Saidiya Hartman, Debbe Hirata, Jason Hirata, Adam Khalil, Zack Khalil, Pope.L, Jason Loebs, Jordan Lord, Balthazar Lovay, Zoey Marks, Park McArthur, Vreni Naess, No Total, Jackson Polys, Lucas Quigley, Nick Raffel, Carissa Rodriguez, Noam Segal, Knut Olaf Sunde

Work organized by Jason Hirata

March 01 through May 12, 2019
Opening: Thurs February 28, 2019, 19 Uhr

Gallery

01. Zoey Marks
Untitled, 2018
Vinyl, 235 x 120 cm
Courtesy the artist

02. Lorel Easterbrooks
Modified maritime plaque for Jason Hirata made and gifted by Lorel Easterbrooks, 2018
Wood, Gold Leaf Paint Finish, Polyurethane
Courtesy of Jason Hirata

03. Jason Loebs
Syncopes, 2005, 2017
Fort Trumbull, New London, CT
Infocus Projector, iPhone 5 / USB charger, Samsung S4 / USB charger, Manfrotto iPhone mount / stand, Lightning

Digital AV Adapter, HDMI cable, custom USB outlet,
birch wood
18 x 20 x 31 in, projection variable
Courtesy the artist and ESSEX STREET, New York

04. Vreni Naess
NO WAR?, 2018
Frame made for Vreni by Nick Raffel, January 2018
Photograph, marker on cardboard, xerox print, buttons,
matteboard, frame
Courtesy the artists

Gallery – Screening room

05. Pope.L
One thing after another (pt. II), 2018
Conversation with Pope.L and Noam Segal
Video documentation of public discussion
HD video, 1h 3min
© Pope.L; courtesy the artist and Mitchell-Innes & Nash,
New York

06. Dora Budor
Benedick, or Else (Night Shift), 2019
Documentation of exhibition at 80 WSE Gallery, New York
HD video, 8min 37s
Courtesy the artist

07. Jordan Lord
After... After... (Access), 2018
HD video, 15min 52s
Camera: Jay Chieh-Chun Lee, Jason Hirata, Jordan Lord,
Ashley Schlafly
Featuring: Jordan Lord, Constantina Zavitsanos (Stimme),

Johanna Hedva (Stimme), Orion Jenkins, Tom Ackers,
Deborah Lord, Angelique White
Produced by Lizzie Warren
Written and Directed by Jordan Lord
Voiceover Recorded at Grand Street Recording by
Jake Lummus
Courtesy the artist

08. No Total
You Should Wake Up Earlier, 2017
A No Total Play with and by Arias Alea, Amelia Bande,
Emma Hedditch, Svetlana Kitto, Jordan Lord, Nia Nottage
Saturday, March 4 & Sunday, March 5, 2017, 7.30 p.m.
Artists Space Books & Talks, 55 Walker Street, New York
HD video, 50min 15s
Courtesy of Artists Space, New York

09. Jim Fletcher, Adam Khalil, Zack Khalil, Jackson Polys
THE INFORMANTS, 2018
Performance by Jim Fletcher
Tuesday, January 16, 2018, Artists Space Books & Talks,
55 Walker Street, New York
Documentation, HD video, 24min 15s
Courtesy of Artists Space, New York

10. Lutz Bacher
FOG (Module), 2019
HD video, 10min 50s
Courtesy the artist and Greene Naftali, New York

11. Lutz Bacher
DANGER (Module), 2019
HD video, 6min 29s
Courtesy the artist and Greene Naftali, New York

Cabinet

12. Carissa Rodriguez
The Maid, 2018
Audio recording of the eponymous poem by Robert Walser
3min 14s
Courtesy the artist

13. Saidiya Hartman
Keynote recorded on October 25, 2018
Audio recording, 25min
Courtesy of Saidiya Hartman and W. W. Norton and
Company, Inc.

14. Lucas Quigley, Lorel Easterbrooks, Jason Hirata
Posters, 2019 – ongoing
Digital inkjet prints

15. Matt Browning
Form Determined, 2019
Black walnut ink, plastic bottles
Courtesy the artist

16. Alex Bienstock
*Artist Jason Hirata chooses items from a library. He exhibits
those items however he wants. He returns them before they
are due.*, 2019
Books from the city library of Nürnberg due on March
28, 2019
Courtesy the artist

17. Matt Browning
Untitled, 2018
Zinc, Copper

Courtesy the artist

18. Park McArthur
Pits, 2018
Sound installation, 3h 37min, Loop
Courtesy the artist and ESSEX STREET, New York

Office

19. Alex Bienstock
Jason Hirata chooses an aesthetically pleasing trashcan for an exhibition and lets it be functional., 2019
Fripa waste basket No. 2340013, daily gallery waste, Kunstverein Nürnberg
Courtesy the artist

Pelican (2019)

Jason Hirata

Pelican

June 29 – July 28, 2019

Summer hours: Thursday - Saturday, 12-6pm
For information: info@svetlanagallery.com

After some anticipation, Svetlana presents Pelican, an exhibition by Jason Hirata. Below, a press release by the artist.

I used to play a game with myself where I'd find something that was just barely noticeable, then look at it until it disappeared. Later, in some kind of a reversal, I learned how to make photographs. My interest in undertaking these activities has declined over time—I almost never do either unless asked.

To make this show, Lorel Easterbrooks and I met in the gallery fairly regularly, guessing that something exhibitable would arise out of our occupation. This was mostly a nighttime activity. We began photographing our attempts at an exhibition, like artworks I thought could be shown, or a few minutes where I unnoticed something on the wall. These photos were made in dim conditions which revealed, through the camera, scenes beyond the thresholds of our vision.

Lorel made this show with me. She is the curator of this

exhibition, but half or more of the ideas in the show are hers.
Later she will write something that more clearly enacts a
curatorial role.

*Jason Hirata, born 1986 in Seattle, WA, lives and works in New York. Hirata
holds a BFA in photography from the University of Washington. This is
the artist's first exhibition in New York. He has recently presented solo
exhibitions at the Kunstverein Nuremberg; Henry Art Gallery, Seattle; and
Muscle Beach, Portland. Later this year, he will present a solo exhibition at
80 Washington Square East, NYU.*

Jason Hirata
Pelican

June 29 - July 28, 2019
Svetlana, New York

Corner, 2019
Foam core wall
83 x 89 inches (211 x 226 cm)

Mural of a Cockroaches Eye, 2019
Acrylic paint on wall
Dimensions variable
(three components: 22 x 47 inches, 55.9 x 119.4 cm;
two components: 3/16 x 1/16 inches)
Edition of 1 + 1 AP

IIII, 2019
Blurred slideshow
Dimensions variable
Edition of 3 + 1 AP

Standoff, 2015
Sheldon Cooper doll
6.5 x 19.5 x 4 inches

Sometimes You're Both (2019)

JASON HIRATA
SOMETIMES YOU'RE BOTH
December 3, 2019 – February 23, 2020

Sometimes 80 Washington Square East hires me to help out when the art they'll be showing has complicated video requirements. I do this kind of work for other galleries too and I also produce videos. This exhibition is made up of six videos I worked on.

Half of the pieces here are artworks and the other half are documentations of artworks. While these documents (which begin with a white title card) are not artworks themselves, they do *represent* artworks and convey an experience of that work. In a similar way, the art on view here, which is not mine, represents my occupation as an artist and conveys an experience of my work.

Making work in this way is something that I've been pursuing for a little over a year. To a greater extent than in my previous shows, this exhibition is a structured viewing of the artworks. The proposition is that *you are in an exhibition by Jason Hirata.*

Thank you to the artists. Thank you to Nicola Lees, Lucas Quigley, Jon Huron, Olivia Andrews, Artists Space, Domingo Castillo, Milan Ther, Cornelia Kastelan, Balthazar Lovay, and Jason Loebs. Thank you to Park McArthur for loaning me the title of this show.

LIST OF WORKS

GALLERY 1

Hannah Black
Ramey and Raymond (80WSE edit), 2019
HD video, 11 minutes
courtesy of the artist

Carissa Rodriguez
The Girls, 1997–2018
SD Video, 37 minutes
courtesy of the artist

GALLERY 4

Hito Steyerl
Unbroken Windows, 2018
HD Video, 10 minutes
courtesy of the artist and Andrew Kreps Gallery

GALLERY 5

Adjua Gargi Nzinga Greaves
Poetry Reading at 222 Bowery, 2017
HD video, 14 minutes
courtesy of the artist and Artists Space

Trajal Harrell
The Return of La Argentina, 2015
as performed at the Annual Friends of Artists Space
Dinner 2017
HD Video, 22 minutes
courtesy of the artist and Artists Space

camera by Iki Nakamura

New Red Order
(Adam Khalil, Zack Khalil, Jackson Polys, Jim Fletcher)
THE INFORMANTS – performance by Jim Fletcher, 2017
HD Video, 24 minutes
courtesy of the artists and Artists Space

Art As Negotiation: Jason Hirata Interviewed by Zoey Lubitz (2020)

Artwork that complexifies the notion of authorship

Jason Hirata's critical practice emerges from a studied approach to the contours of his friendships and jobs, the light in the room, and the food on the menu. He was recently called a "slacker" in the *New York Times*, and there is a certain accuracy in the recognition of his simple gestures' obstinate relation to conventions of productivity.

Before we met, I saw a show he made by writing the names of different foods on construction paper with Sharpie. For a lecture I commissioned from him for the Center for Experimental Lectures, he performed a durational reading of every dish served at every meal for one week at the concentration camp in Puyallup, Washington, where his grandparents were interned during World War II. We started working together because we like to eat, and pleasure, along with form, care, precarity, work, and reproduction, are the subjects of his practice.

—Zoey Lubitz

Zoey Lubitz
In recent solo exhibitions, you have shown works by other artists as well as non-artworks by other people that you had a hand in producing. Some have read this as an acerbic critique of authorship, but I also see this way of working as a representation of your position and practice as a set of professional relationships, dependencies, citations,

friendships—

Jason Hirata
—which are all things that authorship requires, and bodies require, and people require.

I think I am more interested in experimenting within its conditions than criticizing authorship itself. It was Carissa Rodriguez, whose work I am showing at 80WSE, who taught me that: that I *am* authoring something by doing this. She showed me that even when a show of mine contains zero works authored by me, this is not an evacuation of my authorship. I think critical practice is mostly self-critique. So, a goal of this work is to find the authorship in what I am doing and to propose finding the authorship in what your assistant is doing, or what the registrar is doing, or the make-up artist, or the staff. The artwork for me is in the structure and not the object. It's a conveyance of a feeling through a number of supporters, participants, and circumstances.

ZL
I've been thinking about some of your other gestures in these shows, like the image of a pigeon perched on the cornice of a building high above an out-of-focus Manhattan, which you have printed twice at poster size and taped side by side in the window of 80WSE.

JH
The pigeon image comes from a postcard that fell from a vendor near 80WSE at Lucas Quigley's feet one day during a windstorm. The works in the windows allude to a series of posters that Lucas and Lorel Easterbrooks help me make. You are seeing what is almost a poster for that body of work.

ZL

Something other than the original, or the final, is on view. I see the doubling as a formal analogy for the way you show other people's work. The pigeon, like the works on view at 80WSE, gains a particular meaning through its repetition.

JH

The display of artworks is always a negotiation, even when that is obscured. Every time the poster series gets reproduced, it's a unique situation. A version is shown at one place, and it's different the next time it's shown. Not only because everywhere I participate in an exhibition an additional poster is produced from a postcard, but also because that space and that organization of people will have a different need for the posters. Kunstverein Nürnberg sold the poster series in its yearly fundraising as a set, because that's how they imagined people would buy them. For my show at Veronica in Seattle, they sold them as unique prints. At Christian Anderson in Copenhagen, they were a single unique edition comprised of four prints, two of each poster from that show. They are always one hundred percent what the space needs. The window of 80WSE is a space that needs to represent what is going on in the programming of the gallery, or needs to be programming itself.

When I say that the display of artworks is always a negotiation, even when obscured, I mean that there are always a number of outside factors at play, whether they are acknowledged or not. For instance, when we listen to music, it is never in a total vacuum of sound; there is always the sound of your surroundings, the equipment it's coming through or made with, and the sound of yourself breathing.

ZL

This compromised situation of listening is also a formal device in your exhibition at 80WSE: you stream the audio of various videos on view into two of the middle rooms, where it is mixed and has its own life as noise. One of the rooms is lit by the default screensaver of the Apple computer that, I assume, controls the mixing and sending of the audio. Just showing the works together, they interact. So why do you perform this technical operation, an intervention and gesture not used in your earlier exhibition at Kunstverein Nürnberg?

JH

It's a way of being literal. By technically mixing the sounds that are already passively mixing in space, I think it produces a situation where that mixture is acknowledged in a way that I haven't been able to achieve before. It shows that I am presenting a single coherent experience of these works. Also, the structure of presenting these multiple videos as one coherent experience at 80WSE was a curatorial proposal that came from the institution.

There is one project here in these two shows, but there was also a group show at Kunsthalle Fribourg where I got to try this for the first time with Jason Loebs's work. In addition to his hosting the premise with his art and employing me as his assistant, he really theorized the beginning of the project with me.

ZL

Do you feel that my questions now are related to your questions about the work at that time?

JH

No, completely different, because that was a conversation between Loebs and myself about the emotional and psychological experience of making his work together as codependents. We were discussing what it would mean to perform a reversal of power dynamics and psychologies. At 80WSE the conversation has been primarily between me and the people that run that space. The differences come mostly through the people involved, so this project will always present differently.

While I don't think artists are all a certain way, I do think the work often gets asked to do a similar thing: to relate to the world through the commodity form or through objects. There is a lot more to art, and a lot more to life, than objects. Because I am trying to work directly with that structure, I'm rarely sure these days if the art I make is actually visible within the fields of art.

I hadn't really worked for a lot of artists until I moved to New York, which is when I started to help provide some of the reproductive ground that new artwork needs. I was watching art, and it was amazing. I was actually watching it emerge and listening to artists caring for that emergence.

ZL

There is an echo of that in Carissa's and others' critique of the art historical fascination with the newborn and caring for the newborn, of originality.

JH

Which is a critique of the newborn within patrilinear discourse. Forms of exchange want objects to be indifferent, but I want to maintain the connection to the conditions that produce them. In early accounts of the readymade that I have read, it's there. It's as if we figured out how to take these objects people encountered, to enclose them and turn them blank, as if they weren't already authorially inhabited. Like André Breton's slipper-spoon thing. He finds this slipper that looks like a spoon, or is it a spoon that looks like a slipper? He finds it in a flea market, and it becomes *his* found object. But it was clearly something that was made by hand by somebody unknown to him, someone outside of his encounter with that evidence of a creative subjectivity.

ZL

Do you feel like the piss bottles you recently exhibited at Artists Space are your spoon-slipper?

JH

The piss bottles and projectors that were at Artists Space are finished works when they are returned. The show opened in 2019, but all the works are dated 2020, so the actual artwork is the loan, as well as the momentary handling of the object, its momentary keeping, and finally its return. The projectors go back to 80WSE, and the piss bottles are returned to the street. I didn't want their transplantation to be permanent. They are my spoon-slipper!

ZL

Do you always return them?

JH

I usually get them just to look at them and then throw them out. I'm always really worried about them because I hear how they explode, and they might spill. The seal might not be good on them. I have proposed this artwork to people outside the US and have been told that they don't exist there. Maybe at some point I'll try to show them in a place where I'm told they don't exist. Showing them there would entail finding them there, then returning them to where they were found. Anywhere where there are people and bottles, there is the potential for pee in a bottle.

<u>Jason Hirata: Sometimes You're Both</u> *is on view at 80WSE in New York City until February 23.*

Zoey Lubitz is a curator and writer in Brooklyn. She is the co-director of the Center for Experimental Lectures. Recent projects include the California Ideology Reading Group at Wendy's Subway, and the exhibitions *Bangalore Flat* at Home Sweet Home, Bangalore; and *Omnipresence* at The Kitchen in New York City as a Helena Rubinstein Curatorial Fellow in the Whitney Independent Study Program.

Jenna Bliss, Hélène Fauquet, Jesper List Thomsen, Margherita Raso
A collaborative project hosted by Fanta-MLN, Milan with an intervention by Hans-Christian Lotz and a text by Jason Hirata (2020)

24.09 – 17.10.2020
Extended opening days:
Thursday, 24.09.2020 and Friday, 25.09.2020, 15:00 – 21:00
Saturday, 26.09.2020, 12:00 – 19:00

I watch as someone crosses a crevasse. They have improvised a way to cross back and forth, over and over, because they are building a bridge. They act alone and are quiet. I could ask questions, but there is no secrecy in what they are doing. They know I am here. They work slowly and in a meandering way, but never stop. When the bridge is finished they take their tools and cross to the other side. As the quiet subsides, the bridge becomes a feature of the terrain and my attention turns inward.

– Jason Hirata

Édouard Montassut, Paris showing Hélène Fauquet
Fanta-MLN, Milan showing Margherita Raso
FELIX GAUDLITZ, Vienna showing Jenna Bliss
Hot Wheels Athens, Athens showing Jesper List Thomsen

1
Jenna Bliss
Starbucks DNA, 2020
Light box and decal
ø 34 × 10 cm

2
Jenna Bliss
5 Stock/Gangway (chat), 2017 & 2019
Super8mm film and video
90 seconds, loop

3
Jesper List Thomsen
2 to Check a Pulse, 3 to Cross a Border #3, 2019
Eco solvent UV print on PVC on metal frame, acrylic
200 × 140 cm

4
Margherita Raso
Brillamento, 2018
Cast iron
80 × 87 × 28 cm

5
Jesper List Thomsen
2 to Check a Pulse, 3 to Cross a Border #2, 2019
Eco solvent UV print on PVC on metal frame, acrylic
200 × 140 cm

6
Hélène Fauquet
background reflecting the foreground III, 2020

UV print on wood
93 × 48 × 1.3 cm

7
Hélène Fauquet
background reflecting the foreground II, 2020
UV print on wood
90 × 45 × 1.5 cm

8
Margherita Raso
Untitled, 2015
Cast iron
72 × 62 × 25 cm

9
Hélène Fauquet
Untitled I, 2017
Glass dome, silver mirror
40 × 22 × 22 cm

THE ARTISTS' ARTISTS
23 Artists Reflect on 2020 (2020)

To take stock of the past year, *Artforum* asked an international group of artists to select a single exhibition or event that most memorably caught their attention in 2020.

JASON HIRATA
Sydney Schrader (Gandt, New York)

Schrader's *Torus*, 2020, put me in a state of utter disbelief. Displayed for only a few hours on an unusually warm day in February, the artwork consisted of dozens of gray folding banquet tables arranged in two segmented parallel lines on either side of a residential street in Astoria, Queens. The work's title may have alluded to the circular path I traced as I walked its lengths, or to the topology of a coffee cup or even that of a human body, both of which I found sitting on the artwork at various points during my walk, though they were not "part of it." What shocked me about this artwork was its absence of complication and the clarity it brought to the air around it.

From Now in Then (2021)

To open the frame of when an artwork happens and where an exhibition takes place, and to connect the activities of an exhibition with the activities of public and private life, Fanta-MLN presents its 19th exhibition at 21b Via Merano, Milan:

FROM NOW IN THEN

To be visited from the 17th of April to the 5th of June, 2021.

AN EXHIBITION

by Jason Hirata

Of three artworks executed by paid professionals, and developed between the artist and the organizers:

1. *Painted Square*, 2021
	A permanent floor painting, executed by Edilmanca.

2. *Four Framed Portraits*, 2021
	Prints produced by Paolo Nava and framed by Cornice Studio.

3. *Car*, 2021
	A departures service for visitors to be transported from the gallery to a destination of their choosing on the day of the opening and every Saturday thereafter, executed by NCC Milano Services.

A public opening held from 2pm to 9pm on April 17th inaugurates the presentation.

Fanta-MLN is situated in one of the many archways formed by the railroads of Milan. It is a single large room with an arched ceiling. A pair of sliding metal doors open to the southwest and form its only entrance. The space is lit by natural and artificial light and its walls and ceiling are white. An artwork called "Painted Square" covers almost the entire floor in smooth gray floor-paint. As it turns out, the space is wider than it is long, so a section of unpainted concrete stretches along the southeast wall. An artwork called "Four Framed Portraits" hangs on that wall toward the back of the gallery. Four black frames enclose vertical photos of the three gallerists and the artist who are responsible for this exhibition. Curving lines and holograms overlay the photos because they were scanned from the subjects passports. Words like "UNITED" and "OF AMERICA" repeat below the face of one subject, "ITALIANA" can be seen in iridescent purple across the chin of another. All four subjects have brown hair and light skin. One subject has a brooding look on his face, like a model. In one corner is an electrical box with wires that disappear into the concrete wall. In another corner is a single water faucet with a tiny hole below it at floor-level. The limbs of a tree can be seen grazing the edge of the open doorway leading outside. On Saturdays a driver who works for NCC Milano Services sits in a black car on the street. Some days they drive a van, other days a sedan. They were hired to take people away from the gallery. This service is an artwork called "Car".

A Storied Past (2022)

"IL SOGNO DI UNA COSA"

Fanta-MLN
Started in August, 2021

REVISED DRAFT
26 March, 2022

NOAH BARKER, MICHÈLE GRAF & SELINA GRÜTER, JASON HIRATA, CHRISTIAN PHILIPP MÜLLER, ANGHARAD WILLIAMS

The artist, born. 1991 in California. 1987 and 1991 in Zurich. 1986 in Seattle. 1957 in Biel. 1986 in Bangor.

The artist, living and working. In Berlin. In New York and Zurich. In Princeton. In New York and Berlin. In Berlin and Ynys Môn:

OPEN ON:

INT. LIBRARY. LATE AFTERNOON.
A stack of exhibition catalogs. Outside the sky is dim. The occasional raindrop tamps the windowpane. Damp clothes and hair. Late afternoon turns to evening—thumbing through pages of text, image, diagram, notation, index, place, biography. Late afternoon turns to evening and clothes become dry.

EDUCATION

2019-21 Whitney Independent Study Program
2014-16 MA Fine Art, Piet Zwart Institute, Rotterdam
2013 BFA in Media Arts, Zurich University of the Arts
BFA School of the Art Institute of Chicago
2009 BFA in Photography with distinction, University of Washington
BA in Comparative History of Ideas, University

of Washington
1984-89 Kunstakademie Düsseldorf, student
of Prof. Fritz Schwegler. Tutor to Prof. Kasper
König
1982-83 Farbe und Form (F+F), Zürich,
Switzerland, Fine Arts

CUT

INT. GALLERY. MID-MORNING.
Artworks have been dropped off in a mishmash of cardboard
packaging, plastic, and tape which has been removed and
discarded, or saved in a back closet. Artworks have been
hung, mounted, and placed. Track lights, fluorescents,
wall washers. Artworks are put in and taken out. Artworks
remain unfinished. Expectations: surprise, dismay, desire,
realization, forgetting, embarrassment.

SELECTED SOLO EXHIBITIONS

2023 Fanta-MLN, Milan (forthcoming)
Ulrik, New York (forthcoming)
Kantine, Brussels (forthcoming)
2022 Kevin Space, Vienna (forthcoming)
Eraser, Kunstverein Düsseldorf, Düsseldorf
(forthcoming)
4649, Tokyo (forthcoming)
Picture the Others, MOSTYN, Llandudno
2021 *Twilight Brigade Search Engine*, Alienze,
Vienna
Plot, Theta, New York (with Tony Chrenka)
Something is better than nothing, or?, Offsite

Halle für Kunst, Lüneburg
Dream State, Löwengasse, Cologne
The Wig, DREI, Mönchengladbach. With Gianmaria Andreetta, Jason Hirata, Megan Plunkett
Leftovers 3, Kevin Space, Vienna. With Gianmaria Andreetta
High Horse, Kevin Space, Vienna
From Now in Then, Fanta-MLN, Milan
Hergest: Dinas, Josey, Norwich. With Mathis Gasser
Hergest: Trem, Swiss Institute, New York. With Mathis Gasser
2020 *Without the Scales*, Schiefe Zähne, Berlin
Five Summer Stories, Fanta-MLN, Milan
2019 *Sometimes You're Both*, 80WSE Gallery, New York
Pelican, Svetlana, New York. With Lorel Easterbrooks
We walked toward the music and away from the party, Fanta-MLN, Milan
Space #3127, Chattanooga, Tennessee
Witness, Haus zur Liebe, Schaffhausen
Splash, Veronica Project Space, Seattle
25 October 2015—12 May 2019: Work Organized by Jason Hirata, Kunstverein Nürnberg, Nürnberg
Island Mentality, Peak, London
More spaghetti please, comrade, Lodos, Mexico City
Prisoners, Mustafa Hulusi Billboard, London. Selected by Christabel Stewart
2018 *Hergest 4*, Internet Psychoanalysis, LiveInYourHead, Geneva

Leftovers 2, Saliva Saliva, Barcelona. With Gianmaria Andreetta
Scarecrows, LISZT, Berlin
BUG OUT, Schiefe Zähne, Berlin. With Richard Sides and Stuart Middleton
One against All (Uno contro tutti), Whitney ISP Curatorial Program, Whitney Museum of American Art, New York
A Room Like Any Other, Air de Paris, Paris
Every dog has his day, Watch-It Gallery, London
Hergest: Nant, Cell Project Space, London
Contradictory Statements, Fri Art Kunsthalle Fribourg, Fribourg
The Family of Austrians, Oberes Belvedere, Vienna
2017 *LUNAR INTERVAL I*, Swiss Institute/Emily Harvey Foundation, New York
Throws and Catches, Plymouth Rock, Zürich
LEFTOVERS, 3137 at Athens Art Fair, Athens. With Gianmaria Andreetta
Redevelopment of a Soundtrack, Éclair, Berlin
2016 *A Projection in the DDF*, And Now, Dallas
Hergest: Haid, WallRiss, Fribourg
Christian Philipp Müller, Nidwaldner Museum, Stans
The Brink, Henry Art Gallery, Seattle
2015 *Prologue: Divergence Motor/Albatross Alarm*, First Continent, Baltimore
Citadel Spread, Muscle Beach, Portland
Hergest at Rough House, Glasgow International, The Glue Factory, Glasgow
Kanon für 20–30 Frauen, Le Salon Particulier, Freymond-Guth Fine Arts, Zürich
sNewer uContemporary vFine aArt iPaintings

r(Not for Sale), Vachon Gallery, Seattle University, Seattle

2014 *141201-150128*, American Medium, Brooklyn

Glarus Scraping Ball, Kunsthaus Glarus and Klöntal Valley

Contemporary Fine Art Paintings (New) (For Sale), James Harris Gallery, Seattle

Umsetzungen, Galerie Nagel Draxler, Berlin

Optium, The Ledge, Olson Kundig, Seattle

2013 *Optium LH-3m*, Frye Art Museum, Seattle

The End(s) of the Library: Christian Philipp Müller: Elective Affinities, Goethe-Institut, New York

Production Courtyard, Lodos Contemporáneo, Chicago

Fortune tellers make a killing nowadays, The Lombard Method, Birmingham. With Richard Sides

2012 *Bubble Tea*, 4Culture, Seattle

2011 *Quality You've Never Seen*, Hedreen Gallery, The Fair, Vancouver

All Your Base Are Belong to Us, Fred Wildlife, Seattle. With Sol Hashemi

A Conversation, Act Theatre via SOIL, Seattle. With Chauney Peck

31 in Chelsea, Murray Guy, New York. With Fia Backström

2010 *to be like that which you have*, Greg Kucera, Seattle. With Sol Hashemi

Ach wie gut, dass niemand weiss, Artelier Contemporary, Graz

Spring winter? Die Neue Welt, Atelier Augarten

Contemporary/Belvedere, Vienna
Jason Hirata: New Work, James Harris Gallery,
Seattle
Wooden Sculptures, Plasteel, Seattle
2009 *The Gift Shop Presents: Presents*, Henry
Art Gallery, Seattle. With Sol Hashemi and
Claire Cowie
Summer Generally Incidentally Light, Dirty
Shed, Seattle. With Sol Hashemi
March Please Stand By; Stand By Me, Punch
Gallery, Seattle. With Sol Hashemi
C'era una volta un anello…, Galleria Civica di
Modena, Modena
2008 *Resolution*, Galerie Christian Nagel,
Berlin
Show 1, Storage Room, University of
Washington, Seattle. With Sol Hashemi
Cookie Cutter, Orchard, New York, Art in
General, New York
2007 *Die Neue Welt - Eine Art Locus amoenus*,
Kulinarische Kostproben, Gartenpavillon
Stiftspark Melk, Melk
Basics, Kunstmuseum Basel, Museum für
Gegenwartskunst - Emanuel Hoffmann-
Stiftung, Basel
Passé Immédiat, [plug.in], (a show parallel
to the exhibition "Basics", Museum für
Gegenwartskunst - Emanuel Hoffmann-
Stiftung), Basel
2006 *Die Neue Welt - Eine Art Locus amoenus*,
(celebrating Wolfgang Amadeus Mozart's
250th birthday), Kunst im öffentlichen Raum
Niederösterreich, Benediktinerstift Melk,
Melk

Christian Philipp Müller. Portrait of the Museum as a Chair, Buchpräsentation, BAWAG Foundation, Vienna
2005 *Berlin, Deutschland und die Welt*, Galerie Christian Nagel, Berlin
2004 *Im Geschmack der Zeit. Das Werk von Hans und Marlene Poelzig aus heutiger Sicht*, Johann Wolfgang Goethe Universität, Frankfurt am Main, Architekturmuseum Basel. Curated by Christian Philipp Müller
2003 *Spice up Powdermaker*, Social Sciences Building, Queens College, New York
2002 *A Taste for Money*, Galerie Christian Nagel, Cologne
2001 *Humus*, Kulturelle Bodenprobe aus Hamburg, Köln und Luzern, Hochschule für Gestaltung und Kunst, Luzern
2000 *A Sense of Place*, American Fine Arts, New York
1999 *Eine Welt für sich, Ein Projekt rund ums Freihaus in Wien,* Freihaus, Vienna
1998 *Naturalezas Muertas*, Galeria Oliva Arauna, Madrid
Imagetransfer, Galerie Christian Nagel, Cologne
1997 *Was nahe liegt, ist doch so fern,* Kunstverein Hamburg, Hamburg
1995 *News and Gifts*, American Fine Arts, New York
1994 *Tour de Suisse*, Fri-Art Contemporary Art Centre, Fribourg
Showroom, Galleria Massimo De Carlo, Milano
Touring Club, Kunstraum der Universität Lüneburg, Lüneburg

1993 *The Family of Austrians*, Galerie Metropol,
Vienna
45th Venice Biennale, Venice
1992 *A Sense of Friendliness, Mellowness and
Permanence*, American Fine Arts, New York
Vergessene Zukunft/Forgotten Future,
Kunstverein München, Munich
1991 *Feste Werte/Valeurs Fixes*, Palais des
Beaux-Arts, Brussels
1990 *Antwerpen, Linkes Ufer*, Galerie Micheline
Szwajcer, Antwerp
Köln – Düsseldorf, Galerie Christian Nagel,
Cologne
1989 *porte bonheur*, Maison de la Culture et de
la Communication, St. Etienne
1988 *Eh! bien prenons la plume*, Arti et
Amicitiae, Amsterdam
1986 *Carl Theodor's Garten in Düsseldorf-
Hellerhof*, Düsseldorf
*Kleiner Führer durch die ehemalige Kurfürstliche
Gemäldegalerie Düsseldorf*, Kunstakademie
Düsseldorf, Düsseldorf
1984 *Siehe da, ein mögliches Leben hat sich
eingerichtet*, Düsseldorf/Zürich
Wie ein deutsches Wohnzimmer, Rote Fabrik,
F+F, Zürich

CUT TO BLACK, THEN CUT TO:

EXT. COURTYARD. EVENING.
Multiple groups of people, ranging in number from 2 to 6,
sometimes 8. A few people stand alone as well. There must
be hundreds of them. The ground is wet and very dark in

color. Where do they (we) go from here?

SELECTED GROUP EXHIBITIONS

2023 *Ruhr Biennale*, Mannheim (forthcoming)
2022 Apparatus Projects, Chicago
(forthcoming)
Il Sogno Di Una Cosa, Fanta-MLN, Milan
The Wig, Bonner Kunstverein, Bonn
The Wig, MOSTYN, Llandudno
A fool's game played by cowards, As it Stands,
Los Angeles
Burn the Groves, Löwengasse, Köln
*Mit Parallelität von Widersprüchen wird
Komplexes missverständlicher*, Schiefe Zähne,
Berlin
2021 *Othmar Farré, Marta Riniker-Radich,
Gegen Nazis, Angharad Williams*, Die Treppe,
Basel
Spirit Off, Yaby, Madrid
Tourism, Stadtgalerie Bern, Bern
Survey II, touring exhibition, UK
Paradis, Maison R+C, Marseille. Organized by
Marie Angeletti
The Wig, DREI, Mönchengladbach
Paradis, Maison R&C, Marseille
The Things We Make, Lodos, Mexico City
Dora Budor Autoreduction, Progetto, Lecce
Minor Rationalism, Baader-Meinhof, Omaha
Enjoy - the mumok Collection in Change,
mumok, Vienna
sub/dominium, organized by SoiL Thornton,
Château Shatto, Los Angeles

Panoramas and Drones, organized by Anya Komar and Alexander Fleming, New York
at the kitchen table, 1Shanthiroad Studio/ Gallery, Bangalore
PANORAMA, curated by Vincenzo de Bellis, various locations, Procida
Artists' Library: 1989–2021, MACRO, Rome
Aut Vincere, aut mori, Nidwaldner Museum, Winkelriedhaus, Stans
Apt 13's A New Museum's Triennial, Fall River MoCA, Fall River
Fire demands its Fuel, curated by Elisa R. Linn and Lennart Wolf, DREI, Mönchengladbach
SECOND, Fri Art, Fribourg. Curated by Gianmaria Andreetta
Buffers, CFA, Berlin
Reprise, Felix Gaudlitz, Vienna
Taking my Thoughts for a Walk, Dortmunder Kunstverein & UKR, Dortmund
2020 *A# D G# E*, Group show, NOUSMOULES, Vienna
Stay brief, and leave, Fondation Pernod Ricard, Paris
Lady Helen, London. With David Ostrowski
The Phantom Moves Through Space And Through Different Bodies, Kevin Space, Vienna
should we get lunch, I want to burn this place down, Kunstverein Harburger Bahnhof, Hamburg. On the invitation of Phung-Tien Phan
stadtprojektionen IV, St. Gallen
Not working, Kunstverein Munich, Munich
The World is Not Enough, Transart Institute, Berlin. Organized by Paul Niedermayer and

Hanna Stiegeler

A Restless Rendition, Drei, Cologne. Curated by Kathrin Bentele

Kasten, Stadtgalerie Bern, Bern. Curated by Luca Beeler and Cedric Eisenring

2019 *Danica Barboza, Jason Hirata, Yuki Kimura, Duane Linklater*, Artists Space, New York

Art Fashion Pop Up at Airy Clean Artist Space, curated by Alex Bienstock, New York

We Shall Survive in the Memory of Others, Galerie Barbara Weiss, Berlin

phreak, curated by Ido Radon, Institute for Speculative Research, Portland

More, Air de Paris, Paris

Stone Roses 8, Brücke Museum, Dahlem. Curated by Stone Roses

Kreislaufprobleme, Croy Nielsen, Vienna. Curated by Anna Gritz

Same time, same place, twenty years, Berlin

Reset, Kai Matsumiya, New York

Overture, Curated by KRM Mooney, Callicoon Fine Arts, New York

Subsets, Christian Andersen, Copenhagen

2018 *Roots on Wheels*, various locations, Amsterdam. Organized by Root Canal

Constructing Desire: Delerium, Knopf Paul, Berlin. Curated by Gabriela Acha and Antonia Breme

DIESEL WORM, Roskilde Festival, Denmark. Curated by Paul Barsch and Tilman Hornig

Image: Reading, Forde, Geneva

Fantasy is a place where it rains, Fanta-MLN, Milan

October 12 - November 25, 2018, FriArt, Fribourg

curated by Vienna Transit, Gesellschaft für projektive Ästhetik, Georg Kargl, Vienna
CONCENTRATION - a tribute, Gesellschaft für projektive Ästhetik, Georg Kargl, Vienna
Omnipresence, Whitney ISP Curatorial Program, The Kitchen, New York
Don't come in, Berlin. Apartment of and curated by Anna Lucia Nissen and Alex Rathbone
Hack, Kiefholzstraße 402, next to The Yard, Berlin. Organized by Richard Sides
Things We Said, Studio Cybi, Holyhead
2017 *Even my soul is wet*, Kiosk, Geneva. With Lauren Huret and Hunter Longe
Technical Support, SOIL, Seattle
Material Performance: Part II, Jacob Lawrence Gallery, University of Washington, Seattle
Schreibtischuhr, Meyer Kainer, Vienna
Publishing as an Artistic Toolbox: 1989 - 2017, Kunsthalle Wien, Vienna
TISCH, Kiefholzstraße 401, The Yard, Berlin. Organized by Richard Sides and Max Ruf
Kleingeld, Rolando Anselmi, Berlin. Organized by Santiago Taccetti
in relation to a Spectator, Kestner Gesellschaft, Hanover
Natural Histories: Traces of the Political, mumok, Vienna
On The Wall In Chalk Is Written: 2nd Studio for Propositional Cinema Film Festival, Kestner Gesellschaft, Hanover
Metropolis, Simon Lee, New York
Rehearsing Intra-Activity, LISTE Performance Project, Basel

Ephemeroptera, The Hand, Brooklyn
Daisy Chain, JOAN, Los Angeles
Luther und die Avantgarde, Stiftung für Kunst und Kultur e. V., Wittenberg
H O P E, NewScenario.net
Houses are really bodies: escape, defiance and friendship in the writing of Leonora Carrington, Cubitt, London
Scattered Disk, Futura, Prague. Curated by Barbara Sirieix
The New Normal, The Hangar, Beirut
The History Show, Kunstverein in Hamburg, Hamburg
Change of State, Essex Street, New York
2016 *Bubble Tea*, Pane Project, Milan
Se nos cayó el teatro, Lodos, Mexico City
L'état Parfait, Freymond-Guth Fine Arts, Basel
Cos only difference can bring back my friend, curated by km temporar, 83 Pitt St, New York
The Life Intense, W139, Amsterdam
Six Memos for the Next Millennium II, The Cave, Mallorca. Curated by Mario Suardiaz
Kill Your Darlings, Large Kassel, Kassel
開発 *Development*, Okayama Art Summit, curated by Liam Gillick, Okayama
Wet Flannel On My Side, Like A Saddle On A Horse, Transmission Gallery, Glasgow
Features on Radiophrenia, Online radio, Glasgow
Lonesome Wife, curated by Attilia Fattori Franchini, Seventeen, London
Blackmail, Svetlana Gallery, New York
Group Show, Raymond Y.T. Chan, LAc, Seattle
Wir nennen es Ludwig. Das Museum wird 40!,

Museum Ludwig, Köln
Life ist Life, Garret Grimoire, Berlin
Folly, or Vestiges in Greene, Kilroy Metal
Ceiling, Brooklyn
Michael Debatty, Noah Barker, presented by
Exo Exo and Lodos, Exo Exo, Paris
PROCESS, PERFORMANCE, PRESENCE,
Kunstverein Braunschweig, Braunschweig
Whiskers in the name of lilacs, Galerie
Rianne Groen, Rotterdam. Curated by Kevin
Gallagher
Assemble Relatives, TENT, Rotterdam.
Curated by Maaike Gouwenberg
STELLUNG NEHMEN, Kestner Gesellschaft,
Hanover
Ver Lento, Centro de la Imagen, Mexico City
Administrate, Artspeak, Vancouver
Unruly Relations, Kunsthaus Glarus, Glarus
X Bienal de Nicaragua, Nicaragua. Curated by
Oliver Martinez Kandt
Material Art Fair, Lodos Contemporáneo,
Mexico City
CoBK16, Wolfart Project Space, Rotterdam
Ignorance is Rich, Sixty Seven, New York
2015 *ITALY*, Watch-It Gallery, London
Now, At the Latest, EVN Art Collection,
Kunsthalle Krems, Krems
Sounds / Garden, Upominki at Witte de With
Rotterdam Arts Festival, Rotterdam
*to expose, to show, to demonstrate, to inform,
to offer*, Mumok, Vienna
oysters naturel, Veronica, Seattle
neue enden, Kasseler Kunstverein Museum
Fridericianum, Kassel

Europa. Die Zukunft der Geschichte, Kunsthaus
Zürich, Zurich
Pizza Pavillion, New Scenario, Venice
Trouble in Paradise, Bundeskunsthalle Bonn,
Bonn
Cutting Leaves for the Dogs, A Tale of a Tub,
Rotterdam
BNFT, BSMNT, Leipzig
Rundgang '15, HBK Städelschule, Frankfurt am
Main
Under A Thawing Lake, Dark Arts International,
Mexico City
2014 *La référence d'objet n'est pas définie à
une instance d'objet*, galerie Édouard-Manet
de Gennevilliers, Paris. In collaboration with
Richard Sides
House Show, Milcote House, London
d h c m r l c h t d j, Peregrine Program organized
by Lodos, Chicago
Coral Brush Node, Part 1, Fourteen30
Contemporary, Portland
Li With Your Legs, Charlotte Street
Foundation, Kansas City
The End(s) of the Library, Goethe-Institut, New
York
Rooms to Live, Museum of Contemporary Art,
Los Angeles
Fight 15, Center, Berlin. Curated by coeval.gen.
in
*Noah Barker, Benjamin Horns, Hannah Levy,
Carlos Reyes, Eric Veit*, Rear Window, New York
A Place Like This, Kunsthaus Glarus, Glarus
Free Paarking, Free Paarking, St. Louis
Portland 2014, White Box, U of O, % Appendix

Space, Portland
Video Library Vol. 1, Hedreen Gallery, Seattle
Are You Thinking About Atlantis?, curated by
Komplot, Parallel Oaxaca, Oaxaca
*NYC 1993: Experimental Jet Set, Trash and No
Star*, New Museum, New York
Material Art Fair, Lodos Contemporáneo,
Mexico City
No Meaning, 5 Months Space, London
2013 *Wendel! Open your Door*, Cafe Gallery,
London. Organized by The Woodmill
Parallel Processing, Jacob Lawrence Gallery,
University of Washington, Seattle
(You) New Bad Things (Video), RocksBox,
Portland
Dream Island, Royal College of Art, London
2012 *General Practice*, The Woodmill GP,
London
dOCUMENTA (13), Kassel
Unheimliche Reise. Archiv trifft Gegenwart, Art
Space, Zurich
2011 *lieb & teuer*, Kunstverein Tiergarten, Berlin
The Dissolution of Space and Time, Kunstverein
Ludwigsburg, Ludwigsburg. With Laura
Buckley
Bubble Belly, Motel Lucie, Artissima-Lido,
Milan
RCA First Year Exhibition with Richard Sides,
Royal College of Art, Battersea, London
PG – Dip Final Show, Chelsea College of Art
and Design, London
Most Dangerous Toys, SOIL, Seattle
The Conch: A Forum for Critical Discussion,
South London Gallery, London

Pin Mewn Papur with Hannah Lees, The Morgue, Chelsea College of Art and Design, London
PG – Dip Interim Show, Chelsea College of Art and Design, London
Zeit zu handeln!: Werke aus der Sammlung Migros Museum für Gegenwartskunst Zürich, Kunsthalle Krems, Krems
S.A.G.S. Woodmill Artists Group Show, Woodmill, London
Schöne Aussichten, Belvedere, Vienna
Zweite Welten, steirischer herbst 2011, Graz
Public Folklore, Grazer Kunstverein, Graz
Group Affinity, Kunstverein München, München
Residence, Valley and Taylor, Seattle
Sammler-LEIDENSCHAFT, Museum Stift Admont, Admont
(re)designing nature, Städtische Galerie, Bremen
Beziehungsarbeit – Kunst und Institution, Künstlerhaus k/haus, Vienna
COLLECTION - migros museum für gegenwartskunst Zürich, Kunsthalle Krems, Krems
Good to see how busy you've been, Square Gallery, London
Elephants at the Woodmill, Woodmill, London
FMT, Chelsea College of Art and Design, London
Myspace, Chelsea College of Art and Design, London
2010 *School Days: the look of learning*, Lewis Glucksman Gallery, Cork

Chilliwack International Biennial, Chilliwack
Silberkuppe - Under One Umbrella, Bergen
Kunsthall, Bergen
*Der schaffende Mensch. Welten des
Eigensinns*, Regionale 10, Schloss Trautenfels,
Trautenfels
(re)designing nature, Städtische Galerie,
Bremen
Pale Blue Dot, Woodmill, London. Organized by
Richard Sides
Unit 3b Archive Show, Sheffield
The Devil's Necktie, Woodmill, London
S1 Artspace Studio Artists, Exocet,
Manchester
2009 *As If Words Meant Nothing*, Galerie
Christian Nagel, Berlin
PONCHO Invitational, Western Bridge, Seattle
*The Spirit Of The Haus- 20 Jahre Haus der
Kulturen der Welt*, Haus der Kulturen der Welt,
Berlin
BFA Exhibition, Jacob Lawrence Gallery,
University of Washington, Seattle
See This Sound, Lentos Kunstmuseum, Linz
7 x 14, Silberkuppe in KUR, Kunsthalle Baden-
Baden, Baden-Baden
2008 *Principle Hope*, manifesta7, South Tyrol
Summer Institute in Arts and Humanities,
Jacob Lawrence Gallery, University of
Washington
Mighty Tieton, Galeria Dos, Tieton,
Washington
Le Fresnoy, Studio national des arts
contemporains, Tourcoing
2007 *L'Europe en devenir (Partie 1)*, Centre

Culturel Suisse, Paris
*Make Your Own Life: Artists In and Out of
Cologne*, MOCA - Museum of Contemporary
Art - North Miami, Miami
*Make Your Own Life: Artists In and Out of
Cologne*, Henry Art Gallery/University of
Washington, Seattle
SHANDYISMUS Autorenschaft als Genre,
Secession, Vienna
School of Art Open, Jacob Lawrence Gallery,
University of Washington, Seattle
2006 *Around the Corner: Zoe Leonard and
Petra Wunderlich*, Orchard, New York, Art in
General, New York (organized by Christian
Philipp Müller)
*Make Your Own Life: Artists In & Out of
Cologne*, The Power Plant, Toronto
*Make Your Own Life: Artists In & Out of
Cologne*, ICA - Institute of Contemporary Art,
Philadelphia
*Optik Schröder - Werke aus der Sammlung
Alexander Schröder*, Kunstverein
Braunschweig e.V - Haus Salve Hospes,
Braunschweig. Curated by Karola Grässlin
2005 *Projekt Migration*, Kölnischer
Kunstverein, Cologne
*Down the Garden Path: The Artist's Garden
After Modernism*, QMA – Queens Museum of
Art, New York
In den Wäldern, kunsthaus muerz,
Mürzzuschlag Lichtkunst aus Kunstlicht, ZKM
| Zentrum für Kunst und Medientechnologie,
Karlsruhe
At the Mercy of Others: The Politics of Care,

Whitney Museum of American Art, New York
Icestorm, Kunstverein München, Munich
What Business Are You In?, Atlanta
Contemporary Art Center, Atlanta
2004 *Election, American Fine Arts*, New York
*Wiener Linien – Kunst und Stadtbeobachtung
seit 1960*, Wien Museum Karlsplatz, Vienna
2003 *Re-Production 2*, Georg Kargl Fine Arts,
Vienna
Watershed, The Hudson Valley Art Project
2003–2005, Bear Mountain State Park, New
York
2002 *Ökonomien der Zeit*, Migros Museum
Zürich, Zurich, Akademie der Künste, Berlin,
Museum Ludwig, Cologne
2001 *Antagonismus*, Museu d'Art
Contemporani de Barcelona
Sammlung Grässlin, Deichtorhallen Hamburg
1999 *Prepared*, Georg Kargl Fine Arts, Vienna
Minimal-Maximal, Centro Galego de Arte
Contemporanéa, Santiago de Compostela,
Kunsthalle Baden-Baden
1998 *Freie Sicht aufs Mittelmeer*, Kunsthaus
Zürich, Schirn Kunsthalle, Frankfurt/Main
Fast Forward, Kunstverein Hamburg
Review, Georg Kargl Fine Arts, Vienna
1997 *documenta X*, Kassel
SomeThings Never Change, Galleria Massimo
De Carlo, Milan
Landmarks, John Weber Gallery, New York
1996 *nach Weimar*, Neues Museum, Weimar
1995 *Sculpture en plein air*, Môtiers
1994 *Temporary Translations – Sammlung
Schürmann*, Deichtorhallen Hamburg

Double Vision, Swiss Institute, New York
1993 *What Happened to the Institutional Critique*, American Fine Arts, New York
Project Art - DocuMatter, Andrea Rosen Gallery, New York
Kontext Kunst, Neue Galerie am Landesmuseum Joanneum, Graz
1992 *Wohnzimmer/Büro*, Galerie Christian Nagel, Cologne
1991 *Eine Ausstellung mit Fareed Armaly, Cosima von Bonin, Michael Krebber und Christian Philipp Müller*, K-raum Daxer, Munich
1990 *The Message as Medium – Cash Flow und Standard*, Museum in Progress, Vienna
1989 *Jardin-Théatre Bestiarium*, P.S.1 Contemporary Art Center, New York, Teatro Lope de Vega, Sevilla, Confort Moderne, Poitiers

CUT TO:

INT. THEATER. EVENING.
A window at the back of the room lets the last minutes of daylight in. Someone is on stage and an audience sits before them, mesmerized. The artist watches too, and is amazed. It's beautiful. It can't be true that this is theater, stage, fiction.

SOLO PERFORMANCES

2020 *New and recent writing*, Schwabbinggrad, Munich

Eraser, Archivio Conz at KW, Berlin. In collaboration with Richard Sides
Look down at your feet, Subject, Object, Verb, Episode 2 ArtReview Podcast. Ed. Ross Simonini.
2019 *New and recent writing*, Opposition to the commodity, ASP, ICA, London
Now watch this drive pt. 1, Tactical contact, No Bounds Festival, Kelham Island Museum, Sheffield. Curated by Mark Fell and Pedro Rocha
Now watch this drive pt. 1, (Closing) Island Mentality, Peak, London
Snap!, Croy Nielsen, Vienna
Sloppy at Ingar Dragset's 50th Birthday party.
2018 *New and recent writing*, (Closing) Constructing Desire: Delirium, Paul Knopf, Berlin. Curated by Gabriela Acha and Antonia Breme
The Last Resort, Another word for anger, Rotherham
New and recent writing, TALKS at Death Lolz, Elephant and Castle shopping centre, London
Now watch this drive, Clerks Quarters, Bobs Pogo Bar, KW Institute for contemporary art, Berlin
Angharatopia, Care Bare, A right way, Showroom Mama, Rotterdam
2017 *Now watch this drive*, Live-to-air performance at CCA theater, Radiophrenia, Glasgow
Performance at 80WSE Gallery, New York University, New York
Performance at Center for Experimental

Lectures, New York
The Last Resort, Houses are really bodies: escape, defiance and friendship in the writing of Leonora Carrington, Cubitt, London
DIVORCE at Scattered Disc, Futura, Prague. In collaboration with Richard Sides
Breezer, in I have witnessed first time experiences PZI book launch, San Serriffe, Amsterdam
2016 *NO FATE*, TENT, Rotterdam
Hergest: Haid, WallRiss, Fribourg. Site specific performance developed with Mathis Gasser
New and recent writing, Mathis Gasser Book Launch, Centre d'Edition, Geneva
Musical performance with Richard Sides in the Cave, Six Memos for the next millennium, Mallorca
NO FATE, in How to show up?, San Serriffe, Amsterdam. Curated by Elizabeth Graham, Gianmaria Andreetta, Annie Yelensky Goodner
The Last Resort, Priorities, Performance Bar, WORM Rotterdam
Hergest, Rough House, Glue Factory, Glasgow. Site specific performance developed with Mathis Gasser
2015 *A right way*, Girls Like Us, Butchers Tears, Amsterdam
The Last Resort, Foaming at the Mouth, Mezrab, Amsterdam
Do you know there's still a chance for you?, Super in position, November Complex, Hofpoort, Rotterdam
Angharatopia, SIC, Sandberg Critical Studies

Presentation, Amsterdam
A right way, CLFTD, A Tale of a Tub, Rotterdam
Look down at your feet, Rundgang
Städelschule, Frankfurt
THIS ISN'T A SENTENCE, Piet Zwart Institute,
Rotterdam
2014 *Sloppy, Sloppy Mug of Effervescent Gloss*,
Irrelevant Projects Nation Ltd, Library Street,
London
2013 *Destroy your body*, Stop! Look! Listen! Art
Licks Weekend, London
Breezer, Kittler Picnic, Cafe Gallery, London
2012 *Kill the Gibson Veil*, Gallery Vela, London
Fortune tellers make a killing nowadays, South
London Gallery, London. In collaboration with
Richard Sides
2011 *Woodmill* at Aid and Abet, Cambridge

CUT TO:

INT. HANDICAP TOILET STALL. MID-DAY.
There might be a frosted window somewhere beyond
the stall perimeter. Complete silence, until: people young
and old begin to trickle in. Sinks running, toilets flushing,
conversation, music. It's loud.

TEACHING EXPERIENCE

2019– Course development and teaching with
Park McArthur, Tepper Family Endowed Chair,
Rutgers University, New Brunswick, New
Jersey Art & Design Department, Courses

"These are the questions I would ask"; "Some follow up questions"; "Art Is…"; "Art Is…Part II"
2021 Visiting Lecturer, AdBK Nürnberg
2019-21 Visiting Lecturer, class of Josephine Pryde, UdK, Berlin
2016-17 Professor of Artistic Concepts/Art and Public Space, Academy of Fine Arts, Nuremberg
2013-15 Professor for Performative Sculpture, School of Art and Design, Kassel
2011-13 Dean at the School of Art and Design, Kassel
2010 Teaching Assistant to Gregory Schaffer, University of Washington, Seattle, Art, Art History, Design Department, Course "Photography 140"
2009 Teaching Assistant to Ross Sawyers, University of Washington, Seattle, Art, Art History, Design Department, Course "Photography 140"

CUT TO BLACK, THEN FADE INTO:

EXT. BUS STOP. WINTER. MORNING.
Bright early morning sun cuts through painfully chilling air. People waiting for the bus wear hoods, hats and scarves over their heads. They bend at the waist to look around. The bus approaches and the crowd moves toward the curb. Its pace continues as it comes nearer and nearer—it appears the driver has no intention of stopping. Someone in a red jacket darts out into the street waving their arms at the driver.

GUEST LECTURER / VISITING ARTIST

2022 Cardiff Metropolitan University Cardiff,
Wales, Visiting Artist (forthcoming)
New York University, New York, Visiting Artist
with Park McArthur
2021 Zurich University of the Arts, Zurich,
Visiting Artist
2020 Harvard University, Cambridge, MA,
Visiting Artist and Lecture with Park McArthur
The Evergreen State College, Olympia,
Visiting Artist with Park McArthur
2019 New School for Social Research, New
York, Visiting Artist
University of Chicago, Chicago, Visiting Artist
Kunsthochschule Kassel, Kassel, Class
Andrea Büttner, Visiting Artist
Institute Art Gender Nature HGK FHNW,
Basel, Visiting Artist
2017 Artist talk at Tate, St. Ives
2014 Seattle University, Seattle, Artist in
Residence

CUT TO:

INT. 11:45 am. Hotel room.
The door slams closed as the former occupant makes their
way down the hall, bags in tow. The bed is in shambles. Every
towel, tissue paper and cup has been thoroughly soiled.
The garbage can is full of packaging for over the counter
medications. A handful of small bills and coins await the
cleaners on the bedside table. A laptop charger has been
abandoned (not lost) under the bed.

2020- Haus der Wig, Berlin
2021 *Miss Hurry Bring It,* Anna Rubin, 275 Broome Street, New York
2014-2019 Taylor Macklin, http://taylormacklin.com/
2009-14 The Woodmill, London
2007-09 S1 Artspace, Sheffield
2019 *Sometimes You're Both,* 80WSE Gallery, New York
Just Another Story about Leaving, Kunsthaus Glarus, Glarus
Mind, with Lawrence Leaman, Louise Burzoemeny, Hans Christian Lotz, Berlin. Organized with Richard Sides
25 October 2015—12 May 2019: Work Organized by Jason Hirata, Kunstverein Nürnberg, Nürnberg
2018 *Sorry I'm Late. XOXO Echo*, Kölnischer Kunstverein, Köln
2016 *Leigh Tennant. goodies*, Artspeak, Vancouver. With Tarl
CoBK16, Wolfart Project Space, Rotterdam (Group Exhibition)
Fade In: A Tracking Shot, Istituto Svizzero di Roma
2015 *CLFTD*, A Tale of a Tub, Rotterdam (Performance Programme)
2014 Andrew Munks, Milcote House, London (Solo Exhibition)
2011 *There is no solution because there is no problem*, Old Bank, Sheffield. Organized with Richard Sides (Group Exhibition)

Ich verstehe die Trommel nicht mehr: Jan Vorisek and Mathis Altman, Lawrimore Project, Seattle. With Tarl
Raymond Boisjoly, Fourteen30, Portland. With Tarl
Thorbjorn Andersen, Unit 3B, Sheffield. Organized with Richard Sides (Solo Exhibition)
Dick Law, Tarl, Seattle. With Tarl
The Pajama Game, Nepo House, Seattle
2010 *Matthew Green: Kickin at a Coffin Lid*, Duty Free, Seattle

CUT

EXT. NEIGHBORHOOD RIVERSIDE PARK. WEEKDAY AFTERNOON.
The park is quiet enough that your ears might start ringing from the silence. It's summer. You can sit for 40 minutes and not see a soul. This is not a famous park, or a famous part of town, but several people whose work we would all know or have studied lived around here, and used this park. A good number of them still live here. Do you know a park like that?

RESIDENCIES

2020 UKR, Ruhr
2017 *AIR Berlin Alexanderplatz*, Berlin
2015 *Künstlerhäuser Worpswede w/Piet Zwart Institute*, Worpswede
2014 *SUVAIR 2014-15*, Seattle University, Seattle
Face Noises w/ Steve Kado, Artscape Gibraltar

Point, Toronto (NFS Supported)
2011 *Sommerakademie: Group Affinity*,
Kunstverein München, München
2007 *Summer Scholarship*, Pilchuck Glass
School, University of Washington, Pilchuck

CUT TO:

INT. LIVING ROOM. DAY.
A family gathering. It looks like a holiday party. The artist
fixes a plate of holiday foods, some of which are familiar
family recipes. A relative approaches. They aren't getting any
food. Instead they glance over the artist and their plate. They
have a question.

AWARDS

2021 *Swiss Art Award* (nomination), with
Mathis Gasser
Freiraumbeitrag, Art stipend, Canton of Zurich
2020 *Swiss Art Award* (nomination), with
Mathis Gasser
2016 *Kiefer Hablitzel|Göhner Art Prize*, Art
stipend, City of Zurich
2015 *Brink Award*, Henry Art Gallery, Seattle
2014 *New Foundation RPF*, Seattle,
2011 *Shackleton Award*, Vashon Island
2009 *Merit Award*, PONCHO
4Culture Individual Artist Grant, 4Culture,
Seattle
2008 *Milnor Roberts Scholarship*, University of
Washington, Seattle

Mary Gates Research Scholarship for The Summer Institute in Arts and Humanities, University of Washington, Seattle
School of Art Open, Top Juror's Prize, University of Washington, Seattle

WIPE TO:

INT. DESK DRAWER, TOP.
99% of the time it's pretty dark in here. On rare occasions, the drawer has been known to open, in which case its contents become clearly visible: writing utensils, tape, paperclips, scissors, etc. The rest of the time it's more a place of feeling.

PUBLISHED WRITINGS

Eraser, excerpt, UKR Magazine, 2021.

Edit Magazine, Ed. Cathrin Meyer, 2021.

The Last Testament and Will, Exhibition text in response to Max Ruf's Volumen & Kapazität, Die Treppe, 2021.
https://twentyyears.org/marta-riniker-radich

"The Artists' Artists: 23 Artists Reflect on 2020", Jason Hirata, Sydney Schrader (Gandt, New York)" Artforum, December, 2020.

Breezer in Weiss Publications: Anne Turyn publication, June 15, 2020.

"Tears of a Foreman," Mousse Magazine,
Issue 71, April 7, 2020.
https://www.moussemagazine.it/magazine/
tears-of-a-foreman-noah-barker-2020/

Self reliance is a fetish in Vague Magazine. Ed.
Clarke Keatley, Issue 14, March 5, 2020.

Snap! Exhibition text in response to Marta
Rinicker-Radich's Shredding Paper, Twenty
Years Space, Berlin.
https://twentyyears.org/marta-riniker-radich

"Science Fiction" in Entertaining Every
Second, edited by Life of a Craphead,
Calgary: Truck Gallery. http://www.truck.ca/
current-exhibitions/2018/9/7/entertaining-
every-second

"sloppy" in Hard Mag, in collaboration with
Dan Mitchell, London, 2017.

"Prisoners" in DEATH LOLZ, a publication by
Dan Mitchell at Ludlow 38, NY/London, 2017.

"the Octagon Ringmaster", writing
commission for I hope the roof flies off...a
record by Andre Uhl, Berlin, 2017.

"Review of Nymphomaniac", Issue 3, The
Tube, BUS Editions, London/Berlin, 2017.

Scenes in Zeiram, a book project by
Mathis Gasser published by 53 Beck Road,

London, 2017.

"Breezer" in 'I have been witness to first time experiences', edited by Connie Butler published by Piet Zwart Institute, Rotterdam, 2017.

"I thought there was more of me" writing commission in response to the writing of Ioanna Gerakidi. Published in I eat the words and they taste of history, Amsterdam/Athens, 2017.

"Review of FURY", The Tube, Issue 2, BUS Editions, London/Berlin, 2016.

"Dora Budor, " CURA. Magazine," Spring/April, 2016.

"DESTROY YOUR BODY," The Chapess Zine, Issue 8, UK, 2015.

"A right way," LE ROY Issue 3, New Zealand, 2015.

"Sloppy," Prepare for War, Hard Mag Issue 9, UK, In collaboration w/ Dan Mitchell, 2015.

"Closed Fist Open Hand: Thirty Essays about Jeffry Mitchell's Work" edited by Dan Webb and Matthew Offenbacher, Seattle: La Norda Specialo, 2012.

Project Biennale, Another Space UK, Chelsea

College of Art and Design, Sheffield Hallam
University & University of Essex, 2009.

CUT!

INT. BUILDING. DAY. 30-40 YEARS AGO.
A good deal of the people involved in this story may not be
alive yet. This is a different world. It's hard to classify that
difference without over-generalizing, but again, it's a feeling,
and it's noticeable.

Despite that, even today "in the present," one might find that
they can still relate: to these scenes of the past, 30 to 40
years before they were born, 30 to 40 years and more, before
their death, scenes whose possibilities still linger.

SELECTED BIBLIOGRAPHY

Stewart, Christabel. "Death by Cappuccino,"
Tank, Issue 90, Spring 2022. https://
tankmagazine.com/issue-90/features/
curated

Kitnick, Alex. "OPENINGS: JASON HIRATA,"
Artforum, March 2022.
https://www.artforum.com/print/202203/
alex-kitnick-on-jason-hirata-87916

Demircan, Saim. "Remote Working," Art
Monthly, Issue 451, November 2021.

Tenaglia, Francesco. "California Scheming:

Noah Barker at Löwengasse," October
18 2021. https://www.artnews.com/
art-in-america/aia-reviews/noah-barker-
lowengasse-1234607417/

"Who cracks the whip?: Angharad
Williams," Gabriela Acha, Mousse, Issue 76,
Summer, 2021.

Bentley, Kathrin. "Critics' Pick: Angharad
Williams," June 22, 2021.
https://www.artforum.com/picks/angharad-
williams-83265

Editors. "Jason Hirata: From Now
in Then," June 2021. https://www.
contemporaryartlibrary.org/project/jason-
hirata-at-fanta-milan-19003

Editors. "Jason Hirata: 'Frome Now in Then,'"
Moussemagazine.it, April 2021. https://www.
moussemagazine.it/magazine/jason-hirata-
now-fanta-mln-milan-2021/

Editors. "Pee Is Us: Jason Hirata's 'Why Not
Lie?' At Artists Space," Downtown Critic,
February 2021. https://downtowncritic.net/
Pee-Is-Us

Editors. "Jason Hirata: Pelican,"
Contemporary Art Daily, July 2019. https://
www.contemporaryartdaily.com/project/
jason-hirata-at-svetlana-new-york-11789

Demircan, Saim. "Jason Hirata's 'Sometimes
You're Both,'" Art-agenda.com, February,
2020. https://www.art-agenda.com/
criticism/317827/jason-hirata-s-sometimes-
you-re-both

Watlington, Emily. "The Art of Assisting
Other Artists by Jason Hirata," Art in
America, February 21, 2020. https://www.
artnews.com/art-in-america/interviews/
jason-hirata-sometimes-youre-both-80wse-
nyu-1202678605/

Lubitz, Joseph. "Art As Negotiation: Jason
Hirata Interviewed by Joseph Lubitz," BOMB
Magazine, February 18, 2020.
https://bombmagazine.org/articles/art-as-
negotiation-jason-hirata-interviewed/

Fateman, Johanna. "Jason Hirata," 4 columns,
December 2019.
https://4columns.org/fateman-johanna/
artists-space

Farago, Jason. "Artists Space Re-emerges as
an Enduring Downtown Alternative," The New
York Times, December 12, 2019.

Editors. "25 October 2015—12 May 2019: Work
Organized by Jason Hirata," May 2019. https://
www.contemporaryartdaily.com/project/25-
october-2015-12-may-2019-at-kunstverein-
nurnberg-nurnberg-11690

Bentele, Kathrin. "Critics' Pick: 'October 12 - November 25, 2018,'" Artforum.com, November, 2018. https://www.artforum.com/picks/october-12-november-25-2018-77456

Nedo, Kito. "Scarecrows and Bug Out," Taz, June 2018. https://taz.de/!5527470/

 Brülhart, Nicolas. "Contradictory Statements: Michèle Graf and Selina Grüter at Fri Art," May 30, 2018. Brand-New-Life Magazine, https://brand-new-life.org/b-n-l/contradictory-statements/

Lubitz, Joseph. "IMPASSE-ESCAPE" in Omnipresence, New York: Whitney Museum of American Art, 2018, pp. 15–23.

Kenny, Eva. "Photographs of an Unseen Performance" in Under 30 XII. Jeune Art Suisse, Vienna: Verlag für moderne Kunst, October 2017, pp. 20-33.

McLauchlan, Anna. "…WHERE THE ART IS: THE INTERWOVEN SPACES OF RADIOPHRENIA…," Map Magazine,October,2016. http://mapmagazine.co.uk/9945/where-art-interwoven-spaces-radiophrenia/

Beasley, Mark. "Projecting an Island From Another," Mousse Magazine, n. 54, Summer, 2016.

Barsch, Paul and Hornig, Tilman.
"Dychtopotia," Mould Map 4, Cornwall:
Landfill Editions, 2015. https://www.
landfilleditions.com/mould-map-4

Hill, Nan. "Review of November Complex,"
November Complex, July 30, 2015. https://
novembercomplex.hotglue.me/reviewnanhill/

Dupuis, Dorothée. "International Currency,
Lodos / Mexico City," Flash Art, July 24, 2015.
flashartonline.com/2015/07/scott-reeder-
cameron-rowlan d-liam- gillicklodos-mexico-
city/.

Wick, Jacob. "Economies of Resignation," Bad
at Sports, June 19, 2015.

Stephany, Rebecca. "review of Angharatopia,"
Girls Like Us Magazine, Issue 7, 2015.

Tang, Jo-ey. "Critics' Pick: "La référence
d'objet n'est pas définie à une instance d'un
objet"," Artforum.com, January, 2015. https://
www.artforum.com/picks/galerie-edouard-
manet-ecole-municipale-des-beaux-
arts-49721

Manitach, Amanda. "Second Sight," ArtSlant,
November 27, 2013.

Graves, Jennifer Anne. "The Folksy Internet"
The Stranger, August 14, 2013.

Powers, Jessica. "Bubble Fantasies,"
ArtSlant, November, 21, 2011.

Chow, Kat. "Jason Hirata Makes Bubble Tea
into Art," Northwest Asian Weekly, Nov. 10,
2010.

Powers, Jessica. "The Recognitions: The
Best Laid Plans of Jason Hirata," Artslant,
September 20, 2010.

Editors. "Jason Hirata: Shaken Plants"
Pietmondriaan.com, August, 2010. http://
pietmondriaan.com/2010/08/09/jason-hirata/

Graves, Jennifer Anne. "The New Guard," The
Stranger, February 2, 2010.

Kunimatsu, Susan. "Working Up a Sweat:
More than Meets the Eye," International
Examiner, January 21, 2010.

WE FADE TO <u>WHITE</u> AND HOLD HERE AWHILE:

The music of one of JS Bach's 8 children plays. Wilhelm
Friedemann. Friedemann, like the rest of his family, knows
the shame of reason and comfort, and that caution is rarely
unwarranted. We have legitimate reasons to be depressed,
moody, or sad. His music, like he himself, is unsuited to the
world which makes it. Duets for 2 flutes.

Over the music, the following text is displayed as title cards,
one entry after another. Black text on white background:

SELECTED CATALOGS

2007 Christian Philipp Müller: Die Neue Welt
– Eine Art Locus Amœnus, ed. EVN AG, evn
Sammlung, Cologne

Christian Philipp Müller, ed. Philipp
Kaiser, Kunstmuseum Basel, Museum für
Gegenwartskunst, Basel/Ostfildern

2006 Christian Philipp Müller - Portrait of the
Museum as a Chair, BAWAG FOUNDATION
Edition, Band 6, BAWAG FOUNDATION,
Vienna

2003 Ökonomien der Zeit, ed. Hans-
Christian Dany und Astrid Wege, Museum
Ludwig, Cologne

Christian Philipp Müller: Im Geschmack
der Zeit. Das Werk von Hans und Marlene
Poelzig aus heutiger Sicht, ed. Philipp Müller,
Niederlande

2001 Branding the campus, ed. Beatrice von
Bismarck, Richter Verlag, Düsseldorf

1998 MINIMAL MAXIMAL, ed. Peter Friese,
Neues Museum Weserburg Bremen,
Heidelberg

1995 Platzwechsel, Kunsthalle Zürich, Zurich

1994 Kontext Kunst: The Art of the 90's, ed.

Peter Weibel, DuMont, Cologne

1993 What Happened to the Institutional
Critique, American Fine Arts & Co, New York

Stellvertreter/Representatives/
Rappresentanti, Biennale Venedig, Venice

1992 Vergessene Zukunft – Forgotten Future,
Kunstverein München, Munich

Dealing with Art/Für die Galerie, Munich

1991 Feste Werte – Valeurs Fixes, Palais des
Beaux Arts, Brussels

Le Monde Critique, Kunstinsel, Hamburg

Eine Ausstellung mit Fareed Armaly, Cosima
von Bonin, Michael Krebber und Christian
Philipp Müller, K-Raum Daxer, Munich Tabula
Rasa, Biel

1990 The Message as Medium, Vienna
The Köln-Show, Cologne

1989 Jardin-Théatre Bestiarium/
Theatergarten Bestiarium, P.S. 1, New
York; Teatro Lope de Vega, Sevilla; Confort
Moderne, Poitiers,

1988 Eh! bien prenons la plume, Arti et
Amicitae, Amsterdam

1986 Carl Theodor's Garten in Düsseldorf-Hellerhof, Düsseldorf

1984 Siehe da, ein mögliches Leben hat sich eingerichtet, Düsseldorf

The text finishes scrolling long before the flutists cease their carousel. They play the rest of their duets over a white screen before we cut to black to END THE FILM.

Minutes (2022)

Jason Hirata
Minutes
December 3 - January 28

Three artworks open the show. There are four in total.

4. The last artwork is called *Komár* and has the title of *Listen*.
Like others, this artwork has both a name and a title, which
are not confused in this case. *Komár* aka *Listen* is a button
found on the intercom door buzzer. Names identify the
spontaneity of a person while titles tend to describe a social
position, rank, function, relation.

A buzzer is absolutely functional. It can talk, it can listen,
it can let people in. Once inside, a buzzer also lets people
out, or exposes them to the chance and hum of the street.
Perhaps these functional contractions only amplify one's
remove, sort of like something from the past. It never really
repeats, though you do get a feel for it eventually.

3. Two artworks cast shadows in the space and one artwork
is a loan between venue and artist. Usually the borrower
cannot write the terms of their loan, and here, if the debt
is repaid, it becomes absurd material further imbued with
an ownership that supports the self authorship of moi, the
lender. It's a record of the materiality of the show, both in the
physical sense of the objects exhibited and in the relational
sense of the nature of the invitation to exhibit. Its own end
is a tragic reversal of logic and need; but that is not the only
conclusion found or sought by this work.

1 – 2. The shadow artworks appear in two distinct forms, both a kind of recognition. One was a discovery: that a flame has a shadow. The other form falls into an experience of saying something about yourself either being an observed observer or an observer observing. There is no need to choose, and having chosen, one's choice is easily changed.

-Jason Hirata

Jason Hirata lives and works in Princeton, NJ. He was born in Seattle in 1986 and completed his degree at the University of Washington, where he has taught and exhibited. Recent solo exhibitions include Fanta-MLN, Milan; 80WSE, New York; Svetlana, New York; and Kunstverein Nürnberg. His work has been shown at Artists Space, New York; Kai Matsumiya, New York; Fall River MoCA, Massachusetts; and Château Shatto, Los Angeles.

Jason Hirata
Minutes
December 3 - January 28

The Borrowers, 2022
Financial loan
$2,000.00
Price negotiable
(JH010)

Inverted Lighting Scheme, 2015
Lightbulbs, plug adaptors
Dimensions variable
Ed. of 3 + 2 AP
(JH009)

Artwork Name: *Komár*
Artwork Title: *LISTEN*, 2022
Intercom
Dimensions variable
Ed. of 3 + 2 AP
(JH008)

Artwork Name: *Blaise Hirata*
Artwork Title: *Glow*, 2022
Digital C-Print
17 ½ x 14 ¼ in. (44.5 x 36.2 cm.)
Ed. of 5 + 2 AP
(JH007)

Artwork Name: *Blaise Hirata*
Artwork Title: *Shade Flame*, 2022
Digital C-Print

17 ½ x 14 ¼ in. (44.5 x 36.2 cm.)
Ed. of 5 + 2 AP
(JH006)

Artwork Name: *Blaise Hirata*
Artwork Title: *Column*, 2022
Digital C-Print
17 ½ x 14 ¼ in. (44.5 x 36.2 cm.)
Ed. of 5 + 2 AP
(JH003)

Artwork Name: *Blaise Hirata*
Artwork Title: *Who*, 2022
Digital C-Print
17 ½ x 14 ¼ in. (44.5 x 36.2 cm.)
Ed. of 5 + 2 AP
(JH004)

Artwork Name: *Blaise Hirata*
Artwork Title: *Click*, 2022
Digital C-Print
17 ½ x 14 ¼ in. (44.5 x 36.2 cm.)
Ed. of 5 + 2 AP
(JH005)

Up four flights of thick and round wooden stairs sits the gallery called Ulrik behind a shaded black door. It's more or less square, with white walls and black floors, about the size of one of the lined sections of a tennis court. It's a corner unit. Lots of open space and light is communicated through its two windows. The built-in lighting has been shut off to make way for an artwork called "Inverted Lighting Scheme," which replaces the overhead lights with bare white bulbs plugged into each of the room's task-level outlets. As visitors move through the space, their shadows are cast in multiple across all that occupies the room. There are a handful of photographs on the walls which are collectively named "Blaise Hirata". Tightly framed in black, the photos are fairly dark themselves which allows their glazing to reflect much of what surrounds them. The photos are of shadows and candles; smoke; wax; flames; a lighter and a hand. Found in the shadows of the candle is the impression that its flame also casts a darkness like any other. Near the door is a work named "Komár": an intercom that listens continuously to the street below. It's not loud, and there's not always action down there. Mostly it transmits the sound of air, engines, the occasional car horn, and bits of conversation in passing, but it's likely that anything is possible on West 17th street. Finally, there is a white desk with two chairs, which holds a few papers and cards, and a folder that contains a financial contract. That contract is a loan from the artist to the gallery, and an artwork titled "The Borrowers".

Grave Fatura—Paid (2023)

Invoice #: 075
Billing Period: now – Jan 1st 2023
Bill to: **Sleeper Nick and Sleeper Sean**

Jason Hirata
100 Albert Way
Princeton, NJ
jdh.hirata@gmail.com

%
Paid
3002 21st Ave S.   email@paid.exchange
Seattle, WA

Services Rendered:

Grave	deep and heavy. a slowness of considerable weight to the point of hostility	25–45 BPM
Largo	wide, broad. generous, spacious, abundant. unscrupulous. a wind that blows from the side. open sea.	40–60 BPM
Lento	opposed to promptness. loose, not snug. the sway of loose hair.	45–60 BPM
Adagio	slow, stately. in no hurry. provisioned.	66–76 BPM
Adagietto	easy. small.	72–76 BPM
Andante	a walking pace without pretensions. continuous and ordinary.	76–108 BPM
Moderato	controlled, measured. contained within the limits of safety and convenience. one who does not lose control.	108–120 BPM
Allegretto	almost happy. the stall before a plunge, or after an ascendant change.	112–120 BPM
Allegro	bright. moderately demonstrative of the energy that joy brings.	120–156 BPM
Vivace	lively as youth or intense flame. equipped with luxuriant vitality, which has a long life left to live.	156–176 BPM
Presto	quickness as though on loaned time.	168–200 BPM
Prestissimo	persistence of urgency past due.	200+ BPM

Total: 988–1286+ BPM

Total Due: 988–1286+ BPM

Grave Fatura—Billytown (2023)

92

Invoice #: 076
Billing Period: 1 May, 2023

Jason Hirata
Highland Park, NJ
jdh.hirata@gmail.com

Bill to: Billytown
2512 ZB Den Haag, Netherlands   thekitchen@billytown.org
℅ Robbin Heyker

Services Rendered:

Grave	deep and heavy. a slowness of considerable weight to the point of hostility	25–45 BPM
Largo	wide, broad. generous, spacious, abundant. unscrupulous. a wind that blows from the side. open sea.	40–60 BPM
Lento	opposed to promptness. loose, not snug. the sway of loose hair.	45–60 BPM
Adagio	slow, stately. in no hurry. provisioned.	66–76 BPM
Adagietto	easy. small.	72–76 BPM
Andante	a walking pace without pretensions. continuous and ordinary.	76–108 BPM
Moderato	controlled, measured. contained within the limits of safety and convenience. one who does not lose control.	108–120 BPM
Allegretto	almost happy. the stall before a plunge, or after an ascendant change.	112–120 BPM
Allegro	bright. moderately demonstrative of the energy that joy brings.	120–156 BPM
Vivace	lively as youth or intense flame. equipped with luxuriant vitality, which has a long life left to live.	156–176 BPM
Presto	quickness as though on loaned time.	168–200 BPM
Prestissimo	persistence of urgency past due.	200+ BPM

Total: 988–1286+ BPM

Total Due: 988–1286+ BPM

Grave Fatura—Fanta-MLN (2024)

Jason Hirata
Highland Park, NJ
jdh.hirata@gmail.com

Invoice #: 083
Billing Period: 26 May, 2024

Bill to:

FANTA-MLN S.n.c.
di Baldissera, de Risi, e Zenere
Via Amedeo d'Aosta, 3
20129 Milano - Italy

VAT nr: 10501700966
info@fanta-mln.it

Services Rendered:

Grave	deep and heavy. a slowness of considerable weight to the point of hostility	25–45 BPM
Largo	wide, broad. generous, spacious, abundant. unscrupulous. a wind that blows from the side. open sea.	40–60 BPM
Lento	opposed to promptness. loose, not snug. the sway of loose hair.	45–60 BPM
Adagio	slow, stately. in no hurry. provisioned.	66–76 BPM
Adagietto	easy. small.	72–76 BPM
Andante	a walking pace without pretensions. continuous and ordinary.	76–108 BPM
Moderato	controlled, measured. contained within the limits of safety and convenience. one who does not lose control.	108–120 BPM
Allegretto	almost happy. the stall before a plunge, or after an ascendant change.	112–120 BPM
Allegro	bright. moderately demonstrative of the energy that joy brings.	120–156 BPM
Vivace	lively as youth or intense flame. equipped with luxuriant vitality, which has a long life left to live.	156–176 BPM
Presto	quickness as though on loaned time.	168–200 BPM
Prestissimo	persistence of urgency past due.	200+ BPM

Total: 988–1286+ BPM

Total Due: 988–1286+ BPM

fields harrington: non-exhaustive work (2023)

May 7–May 30, 2023
fields harrington
non-exhaustive work

fields harrington presents new research that takes up the figure of the HeLa cell as a signifier of *immortal or non-exhaustive work.*

Immortality is the negated form of mortality: its basis centers mortality as the normative ground which it is different from. If god is that which is immortal, then god is a multiplicity of things which surround mortality and which mortality negates in the wake of its identity formation. Mortality is a totalizing concept on which the definition of immortality is hinged.

A similar organization of ideas can be located in the concept of *freetime* defined as a multitude of activities and endeavors that take place outside the workplace. This definition stems from the idea that capitalism is a totalizing framework in which the world is organized as either directly subject to capitalist production or supportive of it. A totality is any scheme that can explain the entirety of a system in such a complete and exhaustive way.

If "freetime" as a term assumes time as *its* normative ground, then the need for the qualifiers of "free" must come from the fact that time itself is unfree—a common argument made in critiques of capitalism and modernity.

Exhaustion can be defined as the seemingly complete consumption, letting out, consideration of something. In terms of mortal subjects, it has been called a critical buildup of fatigues, from which one has not yet recovered, resulting from a rate of production that exceeds its own reproduction.[1] It is a limit then, after which travel or continuation is impossible. It is the basis from which labor's consideration and accommodation stems—a constituent part of labor's bargaining power. At bare minimum labor power must be reproduced at the rate of its expenditure. And yet it is not. Exhaustion is a condition to which all mortal work is subject. Freetime then, is a vital component to production because it is when reproductive labor takes place.

Non-exhaustive work could be defined in many ways.[2] For our purposes, we will define it as work performed by lives which are themselves not subject to exhaustion: immortal life.

For modern mortal subjects, the antidote to exhaustion is **freetime**: the portion of one's schedule in which all their reproductive needs are expected to be met in excess. This is the regenerative time when the waste products of labor are let out from the human motor. Remembering now that, under capitalism, **freetime** is a concept distinct from time itself because of time's fundamentally **unfree** nature, we can see that time which is fundamentally **free** could reverse the conditions of mortal life and be described as the time of immortal bodies. This means that for the immortal life of the HeLa cell, it is during **unfree** time—their time of capture— that their reproductive needs are met in a gratuitous excess of control and generation that is dictated not by the cellular body in need, but by the research organizations and industrial complexes which enclose, ensnare, and suspend it. In the current state of the world, the cell line's life is contingent upon its capture and the abstract production of value that is derived therein.

This capture enables the extraction of data from the HeLa cell's generational activity. Data is collected, surveilled, modeled and distributed by actors whose interests are fundamentally divergent from the HeLa cell as well as its non-consenting donor, Henrietta Lacks. In accordance with this divergence of interests, images of the HeLa cell were captured and distributed under the direction of George Otto Gey, the cells' original warden, by his lab at Johns Hopkins University. These images demonstrate the material fact of the HeLa cell's robust existence via the medium of photomicrography, which transposes the space of the microcosmos onto the scale of the human world. Along the same transpositional arc the story of the HeLa cell also marks the beginning of an infiltration, which claims ground at the reproductive level whose occupation is still underway and carried out via technologies of abstraction (which have been called names like surveillance capitalism, the control society, and the arsenal of science).

Yet in looking now, at these images from three-quarters-of-a-century past, another meaning of non-exhaustive work emerges. If exhaustive can mean "everything" or "all-encompassing", as in going to great lengths, thorough; then we may understand the non-exhaustion of HeLa cells at work as labor which refuses to exhaust itself. Or put another way, life can recognize life and be cared for, even in spaces that are emphatically labeled workplace. What of the HeLa line's non-exhaustiveness? A non-exhaustive immortality which is incomplete, or which is not everything. An undeniable infectiousness. Reproduction that is both unavoidable and tenacious but also non-totalizing or uncertain; a non-exhaustive existence as an ethical question for death, life, afterlife, and the fictions that separate them. What I mean is that the HeLa cell, whether captured or escaped, is not only incapable of exhausting itself, it is also incapable of inflicting exhaustion on others.

Text by
Jason Hirata and Park McArthur

[1] Alberto Toscano. "Antiphysis/Antipraxis: Universal Exhaustion and the Tragedy of Materiality" Mediations 31.2 (Spring 2018) 125-144. www.mediationsjournal.org/articles/antiphysis-antipraxis

[2] Non-exhaustive work could be called work which considers the workers reproductive needs and does not exhaust them. It could be called work which is performed free of labor, or autonomously. It could be called work that is inexhaustible as a result of a fundamentally incomplete process, which is incapable of total subsumption.

Contingency Lines (2023)

I gathered many ideas from TJ Clark's essay *Painting in the Year Two*[1]. Chief among them has to be that contingency becomes the fundamental material of the artist in the age of modernity. This is so not because the artist is unique or special, but because they become ordinary in this age, which begins with the decline of monarchism and the rise of representational democracy. Private enterprise was not an uncommon practice before, but it is in this moment that it becomes an existential standard of both the individual and the organization. In *Painters and Public Life in Eighteenth-Century Paris*, Thomas Crow recounts the emergence of the early salons as chaotic discursive spaces, situated as they were around the reorganization of revolutionary France. The artist in this era was designated as the one who could "hide in the crowd, unravel the meaning of it all, and turn a profit."[2] The salons mark the first time that both trained and untrained discourse on the arts would cohere in a single space and issue from all social latitudes simultaneously. They also mark the first time that artists were compelled to make work for an audience whose identity they could do nothing more than guess at, in contrast to the court-appointed, and patron-commissioned services that the academy had been invented to pursue. The object of modernity's artistic production (authorized in the age of representational democracy and private enterprise) can be owned by anyone, provided they have the means of purchase. It can also be traded and resold for profit. The art object is newly composed of impersonal work made for, and offered to, no one in particular, which contrasts greatly with the patronage system which this inauguration supplants: art, like any commodity, becomes destined for a certain special no one who can appreciate, or capitalize on, its value. Artistic labor becomes spec work as labor in this age becomes abstractly valuable, and its coerced commoditization becomes a backbone of the modern program. Made-to-spec becomes the general condition of production, a standard that is both enthusiastically adhered to and brutally enforced.

[3]NOAH BARKER, MICHÈLE GRAF & SELINA GRÜTER, JASON HIRATA, CHRISTIAN PHILIPP MÜLLER, ANGHARAD WILLIAMS

SELECTED SOLO EXHIBITIONS

2023 Fanta-MLN, Milan
2022 *Eraser*, Kunstverein Düsseldorf, Düsseldorf
Picture the Others, MOSTYN, Llandudno
2021 *Twilight Brigade Search Engine*, Alienze, Vienna
High Horse, Kevin Space, Vienna
From Now in Then, Fanta-MLN, Milan
2020 *Without the Scales*, Schiefe Zähne, Berlin
Five Summer Stories, Fanta-MLN, Milan
2019 *Sometimes You're Both*, 80WSE Gallery, New York
Island Mentality, Peak, London
More spaghetti please, comrade, Lodos, Mexico City
2018 *BUG OUT*, Schiefe Zähne,

Berlin. With Richard Sides and
Stuart Middleton
One against All (Uno contro tutti),
Whitney ISP Curatorial Program,
Whitney Museum of American Art,
New York
A Room Like Any Other, Air de
Paris, Paris
The Family of Austrians, Oberes
Belvedere, Vienna
2017 *LUNAR INTERVAL I*, Swiss
Institute/Emily Harvey Foundation,
New York
Throws and Catches, Plymouth Rock,
Zürich
LEFTOVERS, 3137 at Athens Art Fair,
Athens. With Gianmaria Andreetta
Redevelopment of a Soundtrack,
Éclair, Berlin
2016 *A Projection in the DDF*, And
Now, Dallas
Christian Philipp Müller,
Nidwaldner Museum, Stans
The Brink, Henry Art Gallery,
Seattle
2015 *Prologue: Divergence Motor/
Albatross Alarm*, First Continent,
Baltimore
Citadel Spread, Muscle Beach,
Portland
Hergest at Rough House, Glasgow
International, The Glue Factory,
Glasgow
Kanon für 20-30 Frauen, Le Salon

When I say 'condition' here, I want to employ the word's meaning as a way of asking after the state or order of things, but also as a way of saying 'stipulation,' because it is within the modern program that production undergoes a state-change from useful and necessary to necessarily speculative, and it is this speculative promise that must be legitimated before any production can take place. While labor takes on the mythic purpose of reproducing everyone— but no one in particular, and always indirectly—it becomes the individual's unique onus, proposed as a right, not to labor after our individual (or collective) means of survival and success, but to barter for them, to refine and sell our labor for the highest possible price, to discover leverage and interest, and perform all the stereotypical actions that issue from and bolster a cut-throat competitive arena.

SELECTED SOLO EXHIBITIONS-CONT.

2014 *141201-150128*, American Medium,
Brooklyn
Glarus Scraping Ball, Kunsthaus
Glarus and Klöntal Valley
Umsetzungen, Galerie Nagel Draxler,
Berlin
2013 *Optium LH-3m*, Frye Art Museum,
Seattle
The End(s) of the Library:
Christian Philipp Müller:
Elective Affinities, Goethe-

Institut, New York
Production Courtyard, Lodos
Contemporáneo, Chicago
*Fortune tellers make a killing
nowadays*, The LombardMethod,
Birmingham. With Richard Sides
2012 *Bubble Tea*, 4Culture, Seattle
2011 *A Conversation*, Act Theatre
via SOIL, Seattle. With Chauney
Peck
31 in Chelsea, Murray Guy, New
York. With Fia Backström
2010 *Spring winter? Die Neue Welt*,
Atelier Augarten Contemporary/
Belvedere, Vienna
Jason Hirata: New Work, James
Harris Gallery, Seattle
2009 *Generally, incidentally, light*,
Dirty Shed, Seattle. With Sol
Hashemi
C'era una volta un anello...,
Galleria Civica di Modena, Modena
2008 *Resolution*, Galerie Christian
Nagel, Berlin
Show 1, Storage Room, University
of Washington, Seattle. With Sol
Hashemi
Cookie Cutter, Orchard, New York,
Art in General, New York
2007 *Basics*, Kunstmuseum Basel,
Museum für Gegenwartskunst –
Emanuel Hoffmann-Stiftung, Basel
2006 *Die Neue Welt – Eine Art Locus
amoenus,* (celebrating Wolfgang

Amadeus Mozart's 250th birthday),
Kunst im öffentlichen Raum
Niederösterreich, Benediktinerstift
Melk, Melk
2005 *Berlin, Deutschland und die
Welt*, Galerie Christian Nagel,
Berlin

The profit motive inaugurated in this early dawn of modernity
is actuated through a number of social value schemas,
namely the trade and relative benefits of private property,
political agency, and cultural/social influence. This motive
rests on the mantle of the individual as a granular unit of
representation, to be rewarded by support from and access
to these schemas, and disciplined via exclusion from them.
Crow and Clark position the artist as an observer with a
personal stake—even a financial stake, if we're direct about
it—in how they interpret and act on their observations. We
can, of course, imagine this mode of engagement applicable
to anyone today, artist or not. Marina Vishmidt expands
on Adorno to say that while this universal interestedness
applies to everyone, the artist foundationally pursues
the routine goal of 'profit' in a way so openly defined that
success means bringing about an end to the system that
enables it.[4] She describes artistic speculation as 'open,'
meaning it can pursue anything including its own demise and
contrasts this with 'closed' speculation, which can imagine
only that which betters the odds of its own survival.

SELECTED SOLO EXHIBITIONS-CONT.

2004 *Im Geschmack der Zeit. Das*

Werk von Hans und Marlene Poelzig aus heutiger Sicht, Johann Wolfgang Goethe Universität, Frankfurt am Main, Architekturmuseum Basel. Curated by Christian Philipp Müller

2003 *Spice up Powdermaker*, Social Sciences Building, Queens College, New York

2002 *A Taste for Money*, Galerie Christian Nagel, Cologne

2001 *Humus, Kulturelle Bodenprobe aus Hamburg, Köln und Luzern,* Hochschule für Gestaltung und Kunst, Luzern

2000 *A Sense of Place*, American Fine Arts, New York

1999 *Eine Welt für sich – Ein Projekt rund ums Freihaus*, Vienna

1998 *Naturalezas Muertas*, Galeria Oliva Arauna, Madrid
Imagetransfer, Galerie Christian Nagel, Cologne

1997 *Was nahe liegt, ist doch so fern*, Kunstverein Hamburg, Hamburg

1997 *Touring Club*, Kunstraum der Universität Lüneburg, Lüneburg

1995 *News and Gifts*, American Fine Arts, New York

1994 *Tour de Suisse*, Fri-Art Contemporary Art Centre, Fribourg
Showroom, Galleria Massimo De Carlo, Milano

1993 *The Family of Austrians,*

Galerie Metropol, Vienna
45th Venice Biennale, Venice
1992 *A Sense of Friendliness, Mellowness and Permanence*, American Fine Arts, New York
Vergessene Zukunft/Forgotten Future, Kunstverein München, Munich
1991 *Feste Werte/Valeurs Fixes*, Palais des Beaux-Arts, Brussels
1990 *Antwerpen, Linkes Ufer*, Galerie Micheline Szwajcer, Antwerp
Köln – Düsseldorf, Galerie Christian Nagel, Cologne
1989 *porte bonheur*, Maison de la Culture et de la Communication, St. Etienne
1988 *Eh! bien prenons la plume*, Arti et Amicitiae, Amsterdam
1986 *Carl Theodor's Garten in Düsseldorf-Hellerhof*, Düsseldorf
Kleiner Führer durch die ehemalige Kurfürstliche Gemäldegalerie Düsseldorf, Kunstakademie Düsseldorf, Düsseldorf
1984 *Siehe da, ein mögliches Leben hat sich eingerichtet*, Düsseldorf/Zürich
Wie ein deutsches Wohnzimmer, Rote Fabrik, F+F, Zürich

TJ Clark's essay *Painting in the Year Two* maps an entanglement at work in Jacques-Louis David's 1793 painting *The Death of Marat,*[5] which debuted in a revolutionary procession of the National Convention that was simultaneous with the beheading of Marie Antoinette. A parade and an execution. In terms of meaning, the two events related to each other indirectly, but in terms of profit, both spectacles were aligned toward the same gain. David's painting of Jean-Paul Marat symbolized, in its representation of the assassinated public figure, the man's faithful devotion to the Jacobin cause of liberal de-monarchization for the sake of the liberty of the individual French citizen. This cause brought the execution of the last queen of France. David himself sat on her own husband's sentencing committee, voting to allocate death by guillotine to the monarch.

At the time of that vote, David was already an established master painter of the court, meaning that his support of the Revolution seems to have been in conflict with the means of self-enrichment that he enjoyed. But we should keep in mind that the French Revolution was not a revolution of the people. It did not seek to apply its values to everyone equally, even if Equality was a named core value among them. It sought to establish the enjoyment of these values as hypothetically available to anyone, provided they have the means of purchase. The Louvre was established (on the revolution's first anniversary) as a museum to exhibit the newly seized art collection of the Crown to the people. While the transformation of this collection from private to public made its enjoyment by the people an enjoyment of use and title, it also publicized—enacted—that enjoyment as an ideal. It trained the public to aspire toward title and toward ownership in the private sense, as a form of reward for individual wealth and its creation. For while the property of the Monarch was becoming that of the people , artistic production was carrying on as it had before, with the aim of enriching the producers, distributors and ideally the clientele—all individually.[6]

EDUCATIONS

2019–21 Whitney Independent Study Program
2014–16 MA Fine Art, Piet Zwart Institute, Rotterdam
2013 BFA in Media Arts, Zurich University of the Arts
BFA School of the Art Institute of Chicago
2009 BFA in Photography with distinction, University of Washington
BA in Comparative History of Ideas, University of Washington
1984–89 Kunstakademie Düsseldorf, student of Prof. Fritz Schwegler. Tutor to Prof. Kasper König
1982–83 Farbe und Form (F+F), Zürich, Fine Arts

We should note that this transformation was underway before the revolution as well. As Dave Beech recounts in *Art and Labour*, the Academy was established to differentiate artistic labor from the craft labor of the guilds. Beech explains that the academy sought to align the characteristics of its labor with that of the courts as it established the ideal of genius as a free and self-determined creative motor to artistic production. The Academy also barred its members from selling their work directly, instead establishing a structured patronage system that was managed to promote the stature of the academy by limiting the spread of its product to only appear alongside the learned distinction of the noble classes. The members of the academy were not of royal blood, yet the horizon of the Academy's aims was to become royal by association. This is obviously in conflict with the law of hereditary privilege that defines monarchical power, and sets up at the very least a contradiction, and at the most a revolution brought on by competing interests coupled with comparative resources.

Even before the academy, it had been the guilds of the Middle Ages that established themselves as miniature corporations that would eventually rival the powers of the rapacious feudal landlords. These corporations were known as bourgs, and have given us the term: *bourgeois*. Where only avoidance, refuge and subservience had been available to the non-landed class, conflict was eventually afforded them as another possible role once their wealth and civic capacity reached a scale comparable to their opponents, the landlords. It was at this time that alignment with the Kings and Queens of the early national monarchies of Europe equipped the guilds with an advantage. In turn, the guilds developed a culture of support—even admiration—for the monarchy, a culture that contrasted with the culture of resistance to the monarchy that had been developed by the landlords. This gain in reciprocal favor between the Crown and the guilds precipitated a subsequent decline in the camp of the landlords, whose indiscriminate taxes, enclosures of common lands and competitive rivalries are now thought to have been responsible for the disarray of the Middle Ages.[7]

Some conjecture on my part: I think that the functional alliance between the Bourgs and the Monarchs may have allowed each party to cooperate in a way that nonetheless forced their interests apart (perhaps this is how things continued to unfold in England as opposed to France). Because of that, I'm not sure if this centuries-long episode represents the incipient commencement of the eventually revolutionary conflict between the Bourgeois and the Monarchy, or if the institutions whose development took this episode as their habitus (such as the Academy and the Third Estate) were in fact the basis of a new and distinctly agonistic form of social organization that invented, in its formation, the foregone conclusion of the monarchy. Such a conclusion would, of course, be necessary when dissensus, competition and speculation became institutionalized at the cultural level because monarchy is a consensus-forcing system of government.

TEACHING EXPERIENCES

2019–24 Course development and teaching with Park McArthur, Tepper Family Endowed Chair, Rutgers University, New Brunswick, New Jersey Art & Design Department, Courses "These are the questions I would ask"; "Some follow up questions"; "Art Is…"; "Art Is...Part II"
2021 Visiting Lecturer, AdBK Nürnberg
2019–21 Visiting Lecturer, class of Josephine Pryde, UdK, Berlin

2016–17 Professor of Artistic Concepts/Art and Public Space, Academy of Fine Arts, Nuremberg
2013–15 Professor for Performative Sculpture, School of Art and Design, Kassel
2011–13 Dean at the School of Art and Design, Kassel
2010 Teaching Assistant to Gregory Schaffer, University of Washington, Seattle, Art, Art History, Design Department, Course "Photography 140"
2009 Teaching Assistant to Ross Sawyers, University of Washington, Seattle, Art, Art History, Design Department, Course "Photography 140"

If, for argument's sake, we say that the end of the monarchy began in the incorporation of the guilds, then we can trace a seam of contingency that runs back and forth over multiple faction lines, flipping its aim as it goes, suturing together multiple intentions and producing a once unspeakably corrosive possibility that became inevitable in its course of amalgamation: The guilds emerged as a way of resisting the direct domination of the landlords and the indirect domination of the monarch, then evolved to amplify monarchical power as a way of flipping the script on the landlords until the monarch himself became their primary opponent, and finally, after the monarch's fall, they became conservators of noble cultural norms, specifically the norm of enrichment.

Perhaps it is because liberty emerges as a popular ideal through the French Revolution that Clark pegs contingency as the materiality of art in the modern period, as art is culturally afforded a degree of separation and autonomy from the strictures of life in general. Contingency necessarily develops in contrast to liberty. Other names for this dichotomy would be autonomy and heteronomy, or freedom and oppression. If contingency is only legible as the negative inverse of liberty (and vice-versa) then both terms must act together to produce what I believe would be called their principle, in Hegelian terms. This principle, the universal that emerges as each term is interchangeably deemed essential and inessential or, as each term subordinates the other, could be called being if we wanted to give it an inflection that veers toward indifference and possibly also liberty. If we want to give it a more interested pronouncement, to cause it to define itself contingently, against and in relation to its others, we might call it survival.

CURATORIAL

2020– Haus der Wig, Berlin
2014–2019 Taylor Macklin, http://taylormacklin.com/
2009–14 The Woodmill, London
2007–09 S1 Artspace, Sheffield
2021 *Miss Hurry Bring It*, Anna Rubin, 275 Broome Street, New York
2019 *Sometimes You're Both*, 80WSE Gallery, New York
Just Another Story about Leaving, Kunsthaus Glarus, Glarus
Mind, with Lawrence Leaman, Louise

Burzoemeny, Hans Christian Lotz, Berlin. Organized with Richard Sides

25 October 2015–12 May 2019: Work Organized by Jason Hirata, Kunstverein Nürnberg, Nürnberg

2018 *Sorry I'm Late. XOXO Echo*, Kölnischer Kunstverein, Köln

2016 *Leigh Tennant. goodies*, Artspeak, Vancouver. With Tarl

CoBK16, Wolfart Project Space, Rotterdam (Group Exhibition)

Fade In: A Tracking Shot, Istituto Svizzero di Roma

2015 *CLFTD*, A Tale of a Tub, Rotterdam (Performance Programme)

2014 Andrew Munks, Milcote House, London (Solo Exhibition)

2011 *There is no solution because there is no problem*, Old Bank, Sheffield. Organized with Richard Sides (Group Exhibition)

Ich verstehe die Trommel nicht mehr: Jan Vorisek and Mathis Altman, Lawrimore Project, Seattle. With Tarl

Raymond Boisjoly, Fourteen30, Portland. With Tarl

Thorbjorn Andersen, Unit 3B, Sheffield. Organized with Richard Sides (Solo Exhibition)

Dick Law, Tarl, Seattle. With Tarl

The Pajama Game, Nepo House, Seattle

2010 *Matthew Green: Kickin at a Coffin Lid*, Duty Free, Seattle

It was after being anointed and authorized as a member of the Académie Royale de Peinture et de Sculpture that Jacques-Louis David found his way to resources and contexts that enabled him to take the liberties that produced his first masterpieces.[8] When King Louis XVI granted him residency in the Louvre, he also happened to marry the daughter of the King's Superintendent of Buildings, who, in turn, helped David secure extra funding for his first state commission, allowing him to travel to Rome where he painted the Oath of the Horatii in 1784. It's in this painting that he bonds the philosophy of Rousseau to the forms of Greco-Roman aesthetics and invents his mature style, employing Roman reference material to render Greek myths and represent modern revolutionary ideals. He developed this style's political resonance through the active years of the French Revolution. His production is daringly symbolic and speculative in how it renders its contemporary world, even going so far—with his representation of the Tennis Court Oath—as to abandon the final oil painting a mere three years after the event because "a sizeable number of the heroes of 1789 had become the villains of 1792."[9]

SELECTED CATALOGS

2007 Christian Philipp Müller: Die Neue Welt – Eine Art Locus Amœnus, ed. EVN AG, evn Sammlung, Cologne Christian Philipp Müller, ed. Philipp Kaiser, Kunstmuseum Basel,

Museum für Gegenwartskunst, Basel/
Ostfildern

2006 Christian Philipp Müller -
Portrait of the Museum as a Chair,
BAWAG FOUNDATION Edition, Band 6,
BAWAG FOUNDATION, Vienna

2003 Ökonomien der Zeit, ed. Hans-
Christian Dany und Astrid Wege,
Museum Ludwig, Cologne
Christian Philipp Müller: Im
Geschmack der Zeit. Das Werk von
Hans und Marlene Poelzig aus
heutiger Sicht, ed. Philipp Müller,
Niederlande

2001 Branding the campus, ed.
Beatrice von Bismarck, Richter
Verlag, Düsseldorf

1998 MINIMAL MAXIMAL, ed. Peter
Friese, Neues Museum Weserburg
Bremen, Heidelberg

1995 Platzwechsel, Kunsthalle
Zürich, Zurich

1994 Kontext Kunst: The Art of the
90's, ed. Peter Weibel, DuMont,
Cologne

1993 What Happened to the
Institutional Critique, American
Fine Arts & Co, New York
Stellvertreter/Representatives/
Rappresentanti, Biennale Venedig,
Venice

1992 Vergessene Zukunft - Forgotten
Future, Kunstverein München,
Munich

Dealing with Art/Für die Galerie,
Munich
1991 Feste Werte – Valeurs Fixes,
Palais des Beaux Arts, Brussels
Le Monde Critique, Kunstinsel,
Hamburg
Eine Ausstellung mit Fareed Armaly,
Cosima von Bonin, Michael Krebber
und Christian Philipp Müller,
K-Raum Daxer, Munich Tabula Rasa,
Biel
1990 The Message as Medium, Vienna
The Köln-Show, Cologne
1989 Jardin-Théatre Bestiarium/
Theatergarten Bestiarium, P.S. 1,
New York; Teatro Lope de Vega,
Sevilla; Confort Moderne, Poitiers
1988 Eh! bien prenons la plume,
Arti et Amicitae, Amsterdam
1986 Carl Theodor's Garten in
Düsseldorf-Hellerhof, Düsseldorf
1984 Siehe da, ein mögliches
Leben hat sich eingerichtet,
Düsseldorf

David traced a bold line through the Revolution and a narrow one out of it. Afterward, he gained appointments as court painter to Napoleon and then, after the dictator's fall, as painter for the restored Bourbon King Louis XVIII, though he decided then to go into self-exile in Brussels where he took a painting student, François-Joseph Navez. Navez would later modernize the Belgian Academy des Beaux Arts and officially add 'Royale' to its name.[10]

I think that in the moment that David, seized by the romance of the Revolution, voted to depose by death his first patron king, he may have found that one could, at the appropriate time and in the appropriate context, wield intellect, inclination, and resource to both end the system of their own enrichment and better their odds of survival in a single act. It's from this moment on that David learns increasingly that his survival is up to him, at times even shamefully so, and always contingently.[11] It's also at this time that we, as a potentially liberated people, began to learn existentially and continue to learn historically, our own dark secrets regarding our survival and its contingency.

For years I have thought that survival was the single most important impulse in the life of an artist, even despite the fact that it can make them (us) utterly disdainful, and even despite the fact that many great artists die relatively young; it is in living and only in living that the work is done, even if living and working is short, soft, boring, egotistic, self-sacrificing, frivolous, painful or improbable, and even if the product of our labor continues to work after our death.

AWARDS

2021 *Swiss Art Award* (nomination),
with Mathis Gasser
Freiraumbeitrag, Art stipend,
Canton of Zurich
2020 *Swiss Art Award* (nomination),
with Mathis Gasser
2016 *Kiefer Hablitzel|Göhner Art
Prize*, Art stipend, City of Zurich
2015 *Brink Award*, Henry Art

Gallery, Seattle
2014 *New Foundation RPF*, Seattle
2011 *Shackleton Award*, Vashon
Island
2009 *Merit Award*, PONCHO
4Culture Individual Artist Grant,
4Culture, Seattle
2008 *Milnor Roberts Scholarship*,
University of Washington, Seattle
*Mary Gates Research Scholarship
for The Summer Institute Arts
and Humanities*, University of
Washington, Seattle
School of Art Open, Top Juror's
Prize, University of Washington,
Seattle

[1] Clark, T. J. *Farewell to an Idea: Episodes from a History of Modernism*, Yale University Press, 1999.

[2] Crow, Thomas E. *Painters and Public Life in Eighteenth-Century Paris*, Yale University Press, 1985. Pidansat de Mairobert quoted in by Crow's, pg. 4

3 The interspersed text in Courier font is excerpted from an artwork I made called *A Storied Past*, 2022. It was originally presented at Fanta-MLN in Milan in the exhibition *Il sogno di una cosa*. The artists named in the artwork were the participating artists of the exhibition, and the CV details that follow are pulled from all of our biographies.

4 See Marina Vishmidt, *Speculation as a Mode of Production* (2019, Brill): Chapter 3-4: The Specialist of Non-Specialism and pg 33-34: "'Negative' and 'positive' liberty are run together for a reason, if we understand human capital ideology to be working with a concept of the social individual defined in terms that favor market rationality. The distinction, however, is important, and it reflects upon the different notions of speculation I am exploring in this project – the open circuit of speculative thought and practice and the closed circuit of speculative capital. More specifically, the 'open' quality is attributable to the indeterminacy of purpose or goal in the vector of speculative thought, whereas the 'closed' refers rather to the teleology of finance as the discovery, expansion and appreciation of capital value, and to capital's enclosures more broadly."

5 See the essay 'Painting in the Year Two', which can be found in *Farewell to an Idea* (1999).

6 See Luc Boltanski and Arnaud Esquerre, *Enrichment: A Critique of Commodities* (2020), translated by Catherine Porter.

7 All these self-interested infractions were soon carried out by the guilds themselves and subsequently used as evidence against them by the academy.

8 David's anointment came after he returned from his 6 year sojourn to Italy as a recipient of the Prix de Rome, which he won in 1774 after three dramatically failed attempts that led the painter to hold an overall resentment of the Academie as an institution.

[9] A line in the Wikipedia article on David by the user "Degouges." At the time of writing, the user has deleted their account. The line was added to the article on February 26, 2009 at 16:30 UTC. ("Degouges" as in Olympe de Gouges, is my guess! – Editor, Rachel Haidu)

The Tennis Court Oath was a vote in which the Third Estate of the Ancien Régime chose to rename themselves the National Assembly and for the continuation of their meetings to be contingent upon the drafting of a liberal constitution by which to govern the nation of France.

[10] François-Joseph Navez, born 1787, died 1869.

[11] Shamefully such as when David exclaimed to Robespierre that were he to be forced to drink the hemlock as Socrates had, David too would imbibe (though of course he didn't, instead staying home with a stomach ache on the day that Robespierre was seized). See David's painting *The Death of Socrates* (1787) where the philosopher meets a boisterous end and his student, Plato, hangs his head in the shame of his own survival.

Dà a chi avaregia (2024)

Jason Hirata
Dà a chi avaregia
Opening: June 19th, 2024
Until September 7th 2024

The exhibition features two parts: some photographs and a sound piece.

The pictures show the place where money got its name. It used to be a temple. In its shadow there was a factory where people made coins. Back then, no one had a name for the small metal pieces. People just said where they came from: the Temple of Juno Moneta. Today the temple has become a small ruin.

Gina Folly took the photos for me. She knows Rome well because she has spent time there. She was planning on going back and knew where the ruins were. She walked all around the site, up and down stairs, through crowds, alleys, and sunbeams. She saw the ruins and the people, and the people saw her. I asked her to take pictures of the four corners of the ruins and their surroundings.

The sound piece is really a sculpture: two metronomes and an invoice. I call it a sculpture because it doesn't have to make sound, but it can. I find that invoices can arrive before or after the work is done. They instruct as much as they record. They are like reference materials. As far as we know, the oldest name ever written down was on an invoice. So, invoices are as old as, or older than, whatever money was before it got its name.

- Jason Hirata -

1.
Dà a chi avaregia, 2024
invoice performed by two mechanical metronomes

2.
Goat Hill, 2024
framed chromogenic print photographed by
Gina Folly and mounted on aluminum
38 x 45 cm framed

3.
Four Corners, 2024
four framed chromogenic prints photographed
by Gina Folly and mounted on aluminum
each 45 x 38 cm framed

4.
Looking at Gina, 2024
two framed chromogenic prints photographed
by Gina Folly and mounted on aluminum
each 38 x 45 cm framed

5.
Comobility, 2024
framed chromogenic print photographed
by Gina Folly and mounted on aluminum
45 x 38 cm framed

6.
Daisy, 2024
framed chromogenic print photographed
by Gina Folly and mounted on aluminum
38 x 45 cm framed

Visual Description:

A long and low building with white walls inside and yellow walls outside has windows and doors that face the setting sun. There is a courtyard with gravel and wisteria. Hung on the walls of the gallery are photos in black frames. They depict ancient stone masonry and the plants that now grow out of it; pathways, stairways, trees, columns; pigeons and people fly, walk, sit, stand, and look; new plants and new structures grow around old ones. There is a clicking sound in the gallery. It comes from two metronomes that sit on the windowsill, each swaying to a different pace. Yesterday they sat on a bench in the courtyard. From time to time they rest silently. Adjacent to the devices is an envelope with an invoice inside. It's been issued by the artist to the gallery and it accounts for a variety of different tempos: *Adagio, Vivace, Allegro, Grave* and on.

25 OCTOBER, 2015 — 12 MAY, 2019
was first presented as a press release for the
exhibition *25 OCTOBER, 2015 — 12 MAY, 2019*, at
Kunstverein Nürnberg in Nürnberg, March 2019.

Pelican
was first presented as a press release for the
exhibition *Pelican*, at Svetlana in New York, June 2019.

Sometimes You're Both
was first presented as a press release for the
exhibition *Sometimes You're Both*, at 80WSE, NYU in
New York, December 2019.

**Art As Negotiation: Jason Hirata Interviewed by
Zoey Lubitz**
was commissioned by and first published by BOMB
Magazine. © BOMB Magazine, New Art Publications,
and its Contributors. All rights reserved. The BOMB
Digital Archive can be viewed at bombmagazine.org.

**Jenna Bliss, Hélène Fauquet, Jesper List
Thomsen, Margherita Raso
A collaborative project hosted by Fanta-MLN,
Milan with an intervention by Hans-Christian Lotz
and a text by Jason Hirata**
was written for the exhibition at Fanta-MLN in Milan,
September 2020.

Excerpt from **THE ARTISTS' ARTISTS - 23 Artists
Reflect on 2020**
originally published in Artforum in December, 2020.

From Now in Then
was first presented as a press release and visual
description of the exhibition *From Now in Then*, at
Fanta-MLN in Milan, April 2021.

A Storied Past
is an artwork that was made for the group exhibition
Il sogno di una cosa, at Fanta-MLN in Milan, March
2022. It combines the curriculum vitae of the
participating artists, presented as a screenplay.

Minutes
was first presented as an artistic statement and
visual description of the exhibition *Minutes*, at Ulrik in
New York, December 2022.

Grave Fatura
is an artwork that was first issued to Paid, Seattle
for issue one of Paywall, a yearly magazine by the
gallery. It was then issued to Billytown, Den Hague,
in the exhibition *Werkgelegenheid / Interruptions &
Coincidence* by Magnus Frederik Clausen and Jason
Hirata in 2023. Finally it was issued to Fanta-MLN,
Milan in 2024 for Hirata's exhibition *Dà a chi avaregia*.

fields harrington: non-exhaustive work
was first presented by KAJE in conjunction with fields
harringtons' exhibition *non-exhaustive work*, at KAJE
in Brooklyn, May 2023.

Contingency Lines
was written for a forthcoming collection of artists'
writings edited by Rachel Haidu and Hannah Feldman
to be published by University of Rochester Press.

Dà a chi avaregia
was first presented as a press release and visual
description of the exhibition *Dà a chi avaregia*, at
Fanta-MLN in Milan, June 2024.

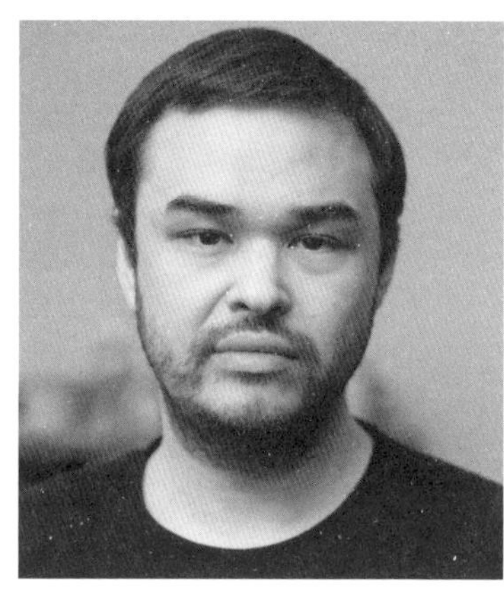

Jason Hirata was born in 1986 in Seattle, Washington, and now lives in Highland Park, New Jersey. He understands need as an instructive force capable of creating solidarity in place of competition. Hirata holds a BFA in Photography from the University of Washington. With Park McArthur he taught at the Mason Gross School of the Arts at Rutgers University from 2019 to 2024. This is the first book dedicated to his practice.

Reliable Copy's annual programme is made possible with support from its Publisher's Circle initiative.

Reliable Copy Publisher's Circle 2024–25 has been supported by:

Ark Foundation for the Arts

Avinash Veeraraghavan

Bilal Javeed

Jason Hirata and Park McArthur in memory of Stacey Milburn

Jaiveer Johal

Mariam Suhail

and those who wish to remain anonymous

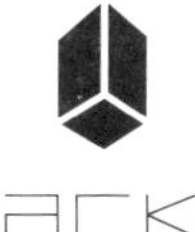

Reliable Copy #14
Supporting Role
By Jason Hirata · 2024

Wiggle Room #2

Reliable Copy is a publishing house
and curatorial practice for works,
projects, and writing by artists.
It was founded in 2018 and is
represented by the artists Nihaal
Faizal and Sarasija Subramanian.

Reliable Copy is a trademark
registered under the partnership
firm Press Works.

Reliable Copy & Press Works,
002, Serena Apartments,
Lloyd Road, Cooke Town,
Bangalore - 560005,
Karnataka, India

www.reliablecopy.org